The Problem of Preaching

FORTRESS RESOURCES FOR PREACHING

The Problem of Preaching

DONALD MACLEOD

FORTRESS PRESS   PHILADELPHIA

Library of Congress Cataloging-in-Publication Data

Macleod, Donald, 1913–
   The problem of preaching.

   (Fortress resources for preaching)
   1. Preaching. I. Title. II. Series.
BV4211.2.M173 1987   251   86–46417
ISBN 0–8006–1145–4

3615C88   Printed in the United States of America   1–1145

Dedicated
to
Princeton Theological Seminary
and those generations of students
1947–1983
who sat in my classrooms
and whose ministries are watched now
with pride and satisfaction

Contents

Preface

This book is not a comprehensive or detailed presentation of homiletical methods or techniques. Such monographs and guidebooks have been and are available in appreciable numbers and hence the need for just another treatise on the subject would be superfluous. These present chapters are a somewhat nervous attempt to supply a partial answer to the contemporary preacher's recurring problem: Who and what am I? Priests and prophets, ministers and missionaries, clergy of all denominations and persuasions have toyed or wrestled at some time or another with this basic and crucial problem and have discovered at least that the more adequate their answers the more purposeful have their witness and service become. These pages are composed in the hope that they will interest and excite other preachers to sense the importance of their identity among the manifold callings of the Christian enterprise. Hopefully, taking the matter from here, they will move on to a fuller and more beneficial understanding.

Parts of this material were given in lectures at several schools. Sections of chapters 2 and 3 were included in the Mullins Lectures at the Southern Baptist Theological Seminary, Louisville, Kentucky; chapters 1, 2, 3, and 5 were the Oliver Lectures on Preaching at the Nazarene Theological Seminary, Kansas City, Missouri; and discrete ideas from all five chapters were included in the Jameson Jones Lectures at Duke University Divinity School.

The author is grateful for the hearing and hospitality given him by the teachers and administrators at these schools: Professor James W. Cox, Louisville Southern Baptist Theological Seminary; President T. C. Sanders, Jr., Professor W. Tracy and staff, Nazarene Theological Seminary; Professor R. Lischer and colleagues, Duke University Divinity School; and especially the students who provided appreciative audiences. A word of grateful appreciation is owed my secretary, Lynn S. Halverson, whose splendid technical expertise put the manuscript into final and highly acceptable form.

Princeton Theological DONALD MACLEOD
Seminary Francis L. Patton Professor
  of Preaching and Worship,
  Emeritus

1
The Preacher:
Identity in Crisis

IDENTIFYING THE PROBLEM

Here are three observations about contemporary preaching, each of which creates for the pulpit more than a passing spasm of apprehension, challenge, and concern.

A teacher of homiletics in an eastern school of theology remarked in a personal letter to me, "I'm tired of defending Protestant preaching with arguments taken from contemporary Roman Catholic books."

In his introduction to a volume of sermons by the late Helmut Thielicke, John W. Doberstein quoted Paul Althaus as saying, regarding the mid-twentieth-century generation of preachers, "People today are not tired of preaching, but of our kind of preaching."

At the outset of his proposal for a doctoral dissertation on preaching at Princeton Theological Seminary, a young Lutheran minister, Gilbert E. Doan, Jr., observed: "American Protestants are losing their confidence in the sermon as an authentic mode of Christian communication, and in the preaching office as an essential mark of the Church. Lay persons are increasingly unwilling to testify that preaching means anything important to them. As a result, ministers feel more and more that their time is better invested elsewhere. The predictable result is preaching of a steadily declining quality, of which the laity have become less and less tolerant."

Faced with allegations such as these, we would be less than honest were we not to rate the current fortunes of preaching as being far from robust. These statements imply that all is not well

11

with the Protestant pulpit in America and that this unhappy situation has been created by more than a shift in the polarization of pastoral responsibilities. Indeed, we need only to listen to a few radio sermons or worship in a cross section of local churches to conclude, as the late Paul Scherer once observed, that there are still some preachers "who aim at nothing and who hit it squarely in the middle."

There are, however, other evidences that underscore the fact that the sore plight of the contemporary pulpit is very serious and disturbingly real. Let us look at several of these as they appear in a variety of situations and forms within the context of the church's life and work today.

First, there is the figure cut by the preacher him- or herself. Strong pulpits have difficulty in finding competent and effective preachers to hold or serve them. When Harry Emerson Fosdick retired from the Riverside pulpit in New York, *Newsweek* magazine ran an article which raised the question: Who among about one hundred eligible candidates would be called to succeed him? That was 1945. Twenty-two years later, when Fosdick's successor was retiring, the question had changed: Where could anyone be found who was eligible to take it at all? Other, and more recent, events indicate that this condition continues.

Committees who are responsible for conference leaders and convention preachers find the lists they can draw from growing shorter and shorter.

Fewer books of sermons are being published by the leading houses and companies. Lay persons no longer read them. Moreover, most preachers refuse to turn their homiletical products into little moral essays which some publishers will sell to an unsuspecting public as daily helps for thin souls.

The drawing power of a distinguished pulpit speaker is minimal today. By contrast we read with a sense of wonder and almost incredulity the accounts of the pulpit ministries in the nineteenth and early twentieth centuries of Joseph Parker, Phillips Brooks, Alexander Maclaren, and John Henry Jowett—to mention only a few—who decade after decade preached to crowded congregations. A caveat, of course, might be raised here in support of the packed stadiums, tabernacles, and tents where modern televangelists hold forth before tens of thousands. But many of these, unfortunately, are flywheels in the complex machinery of the modern communications media or are the product of professionally oriented organizational techniques.

No one expects to go back to those earlier days. The image of the "name preacher" as a community's authoritative voice and perceptive interpreter has, except in a few instances, failed to survive up to the middle of the twentieth century. In fact the great pulpiteer who filled sanctuaries or tabernacles here and there was no evidence of a general healthiness in the church. In truth, these were scattered oases, while in other areas—even in the same city—the performance of the church was less than average. What was more, in many cases when the great preachers retired or died, the large throngs that sat at their feet faded away.

Second, there is the delimited place given to preaching in and by the church itself. On the academic front (for example, in our seminaries), the number of required curriculum hours given to student training in preaching has steadily decreased. When this author began his teaching career in preaching at the leading seminary of the Presbyterian Church, USA, the requirement for the master of theology degree was three courses (each one a 3-unit course) and six sermons in practice preaching practicums (these latter with criticism and evaluation by instructors and members of the class). After three decades the pattern of require-ments is one (3-unit) course and two sermons. Professors of preaching always had to struggle for a reasonable quota of re-quired hours in any academic scramble with mainline depart-ments. Indeed, Lewis Briner, one-time faculty member at McCormick Theological Seminary, remarked with more truth than humor about the attitude of some faculty members to teachers of preaching and practical theology: "They are not real members of the team in any case; they are some kind of retreads that hang around making snide remarks about the impracticality of other disciplines."

On the denominational front, there has been a revival of interest in liturgy, and this is very good. But it can become disproportionate. Many of our church leaders fail to see that the liturgical problem is a crisis in and a search for meaning in worship. This is not to be achieved by the addition of colored lights, pastel shades, or soft music alone, or by what Howard Hageman called "mood building." It lies in a recovery of a theology of worship that underscores preaching. There is good sense to John Calvin's remark, "Without the Word, the Sacrament is but a dumb show; the Word must go before."

On the administrative front, boards and agencies in the headquarters of various denominations are, at present, highly programmed and project-conscious. Each has a program to be put across. And many synods and presbyteries have become merely the extensions of program agencies. For example, a large percentage of the Sundays of the Christian year have been invaded by denominational agencies; Sunday after Sunday is designated by packages of publicity materials—Youth Sunday, United Nations Sunday, I Am an American Day, Christian College Sunday, Economic Justice Sunday, World Order and Peace Sunday, and so on. Indeed, a young minister in the Presbytery of Chicago wrote, "If I followed all the Sunday designations from the head offices of my Church I'd have no time to preach the Gospel!"

On the parish front, the concept of the minister as "pastor-director" (which was a label Richard Niebuhr used to describe a disease) has somehow stuck. Instead of "preacher-pastor," a more appropriate term minted by Eugene Carson Blake, we got "the organization man." Keep everything moving. Make sure everybody is busy. And in this frantic hurly-burly, the minister never backs off often enough or long enough to gain a clear perspective on things or to arrange priorities among those tasks he or she is expected to do. Many modern preachers, as Daniel Jenkins

lamented, "speak of themselves as 'big brothers' who exist to provide 'helping hands' and to diffuse 'radiant cheerfulness' to their
people." They have so misunderstood ministry that many fail "to
relate the Word of God to the human condition" and instead try
"to feed their people out of their own resources."[1]

There are some ministers, however, who have gone to the
other extreme; they rest upon dead center. Things are quiet in
their parish. They have found a comfortable berth. Nothing prophetic is ever said. Nothing revolutionary ever happens. All is
safe in the ark called status quo. Such types have succumbed to
the last of David Christie's three ministerial temptations: "To
shine; to whine; or to recline."

It would be easy to point to one or all of the foregoing features
or conditions and to say that "because of this or that, preaching
is through." And there would be a bit of truth in it. But these are
not causes. They are symptoms of a disease; and it originates not
in the parish or congregation, but with the ministry itself. It
exists among ministers who have lost faith in preaching. Preaching has failed because somewhere preachers have failed. And
their failure has gone hand in hand with a misunderstanding of
what the ministry of preaching means and involves.

This misunderstanding of the ministry of preaching takes various forms and needs to be given more than a passing notice. It
can be attributed to a parochial conception of what effective
preaching is and demands. Some preachers have a minimal
respect for preaching because the only preaching they knew in
their early and formative years was, at best, mediocre. It had
little or no impact upon the community. It had no inspirational
lift and scant teaching value. Over a century ago, Emerson,
experiencing such preaching, wrote in his *Journal:*

> At church today I felt how unequal is the match of words against
> things. Cease, O thou unauthorized talker, to prate of consolation,
> resignation, and spiritual joys in neat and balanced sentences. For I
> know these people who sit below . . . for care and calamity are
> THINGS to them. There is the shopkeeper whose daughter has gone
> mad, and he is looking up through his spectacles to see what you have

for him. Here is my friend whose pupils are leaving him and he knows
not where to turn his hand next. Here is the stagecoach driver who has
jaundice and cannot get well. . . . Speak, thing, or hold thy peace.[2]

A misunderstanding exists in the mind of the preacher who is
continually anxious for concrete, numerical results. Here we
have the statistically minded minister who is a walking incarna-
tion of the Gallup poll. At the end of the calendar year, he or she
tabulates so many counseling sessions held, marriages saved,
alcoholics straightened out, and so forth; and all these are com-
puted with graphs over against national aggregates and aver-
ages. But when it comes to pulpit work, there cannot be any
concrete accounting of the number of souls who were inspired,
moved, or reconciled. Hence, preaching is relegated to the gray
area of the unidentifiable and immeasurable.

This misunderstanding is affected by the large proportion of
preachers who succumb to the boredom and slump of the middle
years. The late Carlyle Marney described it clearly when he
wrote, "Something threatening and un-manning happens to us
in our most vital years. Any pastor is a quite different person
twenty years after leaving seminary to go to his first village. . . .
By and large we become shaken reeds, smoking lamps, earthen
vessels, untempered mortar, spent arrows. Ten to twenty years
out on our pilgrimage and not many of us are *viator*, 'man on a
journey.' We have become blessers of a culture." Hence, you get
the preacher who said to this author, "My faithful group comes
regardless. They are no more there for good preaching or bad.
They all say, 'I enjoyed it very much.' So I gave up trying." Is it too
much to say parenthetically, "Such defeatism or contentment
with mediocrity has never built up a church"?

Then there are preachers who have simply "lost their souls."
Torn by parish tensions, social and economic pressures, macer-
ated from pushing multiple plans and lively projects, they have
no time to be still and know that God is God. Hence, they go
round and round upon a plateau from which there is no sign of
further ascent. Or, to change the metaphor, they have become

dried up or suffer from burn-out. And, therefore, in a desperate hour, maybe ten o'clock on Saturday evening, they reach frantically for that fictitious volume "Pithy Points for Played-out Preachers." And so we might go on multiplying cases and examples, but what disturbs us more than these casts of mind and dispositions is the kind of preaching they produce.

Common honesty among us indicates that what many congregations are receiving or are forced to listen to on Sunday morning is *irrelevant*. In many instances it consists of heavy biblical or theological materials gleaned from commentaries, but not sorted out and digested by the preacher, and, hence, fails to come to grips with the critical issues of our common life.

Such preaching is *moralistic*. It is the equivalent of moral chats with no peculiar ethical sanction other than what average human decency prescribes. Sometimes it is sentimental; often it is tiringly folksy. Its kerygma may not rise very far above "be kind to grandmother and the cat." High on its festivals of the church year are Mother's Day, Rural Life Sunday, I Am an American Day, and so forth. Rose petals inevitably get into the Sacrament of Baptism or mingle with the liturgy of the burial of the dead.

Such preaching is *lifeless*. There is no connection between the human condition and the vitality of spiritual concern. No gospel is advocated or witnessed to with an urgency that accompanies a matter of life and death. Charles Kingsley used to lean over the pulpit on Sunday morning and say, "Here we are again to talk about what is really going on in your soul and mine." But so frequently today what is said and how it is said merely leads hearers to shrug it off. After decades of hearing classroom sermons, William M. Macgregor of Glasgow said, "There are only three kinds of sermons: those that are dull; those that are duller; and those that are inconceivably dull." Indeed, a Methodist bishop said of a preacher in his district, "He's supernaturally dull. No one could be that dull without divine aid!"

Such preaching is *uninformed*. In our day, radio, television, and every other form of telecommunications have enhanced our general knowledge, sharpened our perception, and brought experts in many fields into our living rooms. Never has the pulpit had more competition and never has it been more necessary for the preacher to be perfectly sure of his or her materials—soundness, accuracy, reasonableness, and truth unquestionable. Some years ago, during an economic and industrial recession, congregational enrollments were falling off and many preachers were on a weekly "economic kick" in their sermons. The Reverend John S. Bonnell of the Fifth Avenue Presbyterian Church, New York City, was addressing an assembly of students preparing for the Christian ministry and he warned, "No sharp-minded business man wants to come to church on Sunday to hear just another ignorant analysis of economic theory."

If Christian preaching be no more than these observations would suggest, then let it die. Indeed it deserves to die. It is not worth saving. What is more, any attempt to make a case for this kind of thing would be merely an attempt to save our jobs or to perpetuate a tradition which by this date in the twentieth century has outlived its usefulness. Moreover, many self-help notions reduce the problem to the category of the means and methods of communication, in which case it cannot compete favorably or successfully with the advanced and expert skills of this technological age.

But, on serious and second thought, Christian preaching will not permit us to dismiss it so easily. Our tendency has been to base our judgments of preaching upon the diseases that beset it and within the perspective of the present alone. This might be appropriate if preaching were merely a matter of techniques. Our criteria would then be selected from the basic mechanics of communications theory and would include vocal quality, audience contact, articulation, gestures, and the like. But any discussion confined to such factors would limit its scope, important as they are in its execution. No one who explores preaching seriously can disregard its history (its beginnings with the Old Testament prophets, its flourishing in the Synoptic Gospels and Acts of the Apostles, its daring thrust into the inclement atmosphere of the pagan world, its trumpeting of the message of the Reformation, its dynamic voice in the evangelical revivals), its theology (Professor Herbert H. Farmer of Cambridge said, "Whoso says Christianity, says preaching"), or its involvement in the mission of the church (ordinands who hear this declaration when they rise from their knees, "Take thou authority to preach the Word and administer the Sacraments").

In view of these considerations, the crisis in preaching today is not merely a matter of a sermon having or not having three points and a conclusion. It is bound up with *who* the preacher is, with *what* this enterprise is in which the preacher is engaged and involved, and *why*, that is, for whose sake it is done anyway. Who, what, and why are inseparable in any discussion of preaching, for each of them incorporates the matter of identity so important to defining both our understanding and our strategy in our Christian witness in this day and to our generation.

THE IDENTITY OF THE PREACHER

It is to queries such as those above that writers of other times on the identity of the preacher and the integrity of preaching have directed themselves. Peter T. Forsyth, in one of the finest books on the theology of preaching, said, "You are to preach the Gospel to the Church so that with the Church you may bring the Gospel to the world."[3] Douglas Webster, former professor of missions at Selly Oaks and latterly a canon of St. Paul's, London, wrote, "The Church is called to be Christ's working body in today's working world."[4] And Robert A. Guelich, in an article entitled "On Being a Minister of the Word," wrote of the church as a gathering "around a minister of the Word in order to meet the Living Word."[5] These tremendous concepts impress upon us the seriousness of our theme and send us back to look at ourselves as preachers, at the church, at its mission, and we are challenged by two pressing questions:

First, is the contemporary preacher really sure of who he or she is and what the job or calling entails? Are identity and integrity in the last analysis personal issues? What is the yardstick, if any, by which our pulpit effectiveness is measured? Paul Clifford put into doggerel verse what is all too often the image or conception of the role of the contemporary preacher:

> Like a corporation
> Works the Church of God.
> Brothers, we are treading
> Where Henry Ford has trod;
> We are all mass-minded,
> One huge body we;
> Planning world salvation
> Through the hierarchy.[6]

Second, is the enterprise in which the preacher's role is played a center of dynamic and purposeful action? Is something really happening in the vital areas of the church's life, something creative? Is there a contagion, a dynamic, or a ferment? Can the preacher see its effect upon the community? Or, are the well-worn clichés of the 1960s and 1970s still true—"the ghetto complex," "the establishment," or "the Gothic monolith"?

These are searching and probing questions. Directly and forcibly they put the preacher at the center of things. His or hers is an inside job and together with the church they must emerge as creative and redemptive forces in the world. This indicates how crucial the role of the preacher is and how it must haunt the thinking of those who take their calling seriously.

Someone, however, asks: What about the laity and the preacher's relationship to them? There is a renewed emphasis today upon the importance and significance of the laity. They are, as someone said, the church's "frozen assets." And any effort to retrieve or recapture such resources is to be commended as a recovery of a lost plank in the Reformed platform. Some years ago, Margaret Frakes of *The Christian Century* referred to the laity as "the primary agency through which the Church witnesses in and to the world." But here we must not overlook the fact that in all this activity the initiative lies with us as ministers. This modern emphasis upon the laity will get nowhere unless men and women are grounded and articulate in a basic understanding of the Christian faith. God gave the minister to the church to be God's servant. As Charles Duthie pointed out, "He [the minister] does not derive his authority from the Church, but from God; the Church, however, is the sphere of his service, so that under Christ he is the servant of the Church. If the Church is the Body of Christ, then the minister is called upon to make it an effective body."[7] In other words, the church—which consists of a congregation of laity—will be what the minister makes it. Or, to quote Forsyth again, "The ministry does not have to reform the world, but to create a Church for the world's reformation." Or, further, he wrote: "If the Church does not have its chief believers in the pulpit, it is unfortunate."[8]

This accounts, at least in part, for the lack of creativity among many ministers today. It is so often the case that there are more potentially great believers in the pew than in the pulpit. This happens whenever the pulpit succumbs to the machinery of organized religion and to the elevation of means over ends. This is why so many ministers are miserable much of the time. They become restive and restless. The moderator of one of our denominations, after visits to many presbyteries and synods, declared that the most common of his concerns was "a ministry who had lost a sense of who and what they are." It is akin to the oft-quoted remark of Willie Loman's son about his late father in Arthur Miller's *Death of a Salesman*, "He never knew who he was." Donald Bloesch, in an article in *The Reformed Journal*, echoes a similar observation regarding the church's ministers as he sees them: "They are suffering today from a crisis of identity. They no longer understand their true role. They see themselves as counsellors, administrators, and public relations people, but not as ambassadors of Christ and Shepherds of a flock."[9] Such words touch a sensitive nerve in the ministry of today. Indeed, whenever there is a slump in the quality and significance of preaching, it is due largely to preachers who are unsure of who and what they are. Imagine our putting such a question to Chrysostom, Thomas Chalmers, Brooks, George W. Truett, or Fosdick? Whenever preachers lose a true sense of who they are, of their real identity, and become peddlers of temporary panaceas, or patchers up of quarrels, or psychiatric neophytes without a couch, then what they say and stand for ceases to count.

The preacher's loss of a clear sense of identity among the laity is a danger also in the handling of the various facets of the ministry as vocationally conceived today. It is easy to lose one's sense of proportion and to label some one activity or emphasis as the sine qua non of ministry. Hence, we hear parishioners say, "He was a good administrator, but he was no student of the Bible." Or, "She was a kind pastor, but lacked a prophetic message." Or, as it was said of one minister, "He suffered from foot and mouth disease; he wouldn't visit and he couldn't preach." Probably one of the most common astigmatisms among younger preachers currently is to magnify the counseling room at the expense of the pulpit. No one of us should downgrade any one aspect of Christian ministry, for only wholeness, proportion, and a balanced perspective among multiple responsibilities can make any ministry adequate for these challenging days.

There is, on the other hand, some truth in what Edwin T. Dahlberg said when he was president of the National Council of Churches; he warned today's religious leaders to regain a special sense of responsibility in preaching the Gospel. He declared to a group of preachers in a midwestern city:

> The increasingly heavy load of pastoral counselling should be possibly a warning to us that we have not been preaching an adequate Gospel. We cannot substitute counselling for conversion. Conversion means clearing up guilt and fears at one stroke in the acceptance of the grace of God in Christ. It means becoming religiously self-reliant with no need always to be weeping on somebody else's shoulder.

Then he added:

> The counselling process has given the impression, especially among

young people, that it is their duty to have a problem, to be confused and mixed-up, in order to be in style psychologically.

So much for diagnosis. Now, a word in summary: we have seen that preaching—once the strongest factor in the program of the Protestant Reformation—is in a period of crisis. This is seen in the figure cut by the preacher him- or herself and in the downgrading of the pulpit in the face of new aspects of ministry. Our lay people are hearing bad preaching and are inclined to write the pulpit off. Shortsightedly, many preachers see their role as being caught in a vicious circle or suffering from the law of diminishing returns. No one seems to see preaching in the right perspective—its history, its theology, and its place in the worship and mission of the church. Thomas F. Torrance writes, "Kerygma means both the thing preached and the preaching of it in one."[10] Preaching cannot be discussed apart from the preacher. It is time, then, for us to discover/rediscover the preacher: Who is he or she? In what are they involved? And why?

2
The Preacher's Agenda:
Word

WHAT, REALLY, IS PREACHING?

Books on preaching are legion. Indeed, unless someone breaks new ground, there should be a moratorium on books about homiletics for at least a decade. It is folly to talk about twelve reasons for the use of a text, the proper length of an introduction, or five tests of a good conclusion in a day when the very raison d'être of preaching is suspect and the impact of the pulpit as an effective means of teaching or even of communication is questioned. Our need is for books about the preacher. These are not too plentiful; moreover, many are of the wrong kind.

The typical discussion of the preacher deals with him or her as pastor, counselor, administrator, and so forth, which leads to a fragmented conception or interpretation of the preacher's role and responsibility. This is aggravated further by the contemporary development of specialized ministries in which we get a minister of education, a minister of visitation, a minister of pastoral outreach, and so on. But the preaching minister: Who is he? Who is she? Who is the preacher? Specialized ministries are able to marshal concrete statistics, set up graphs, tally gains or losses, and talk in terms of totals—the number of hospital calls made, of membership gains, of budget percentages—whereas the ministry of preaching cannot be measured in terms of numerical scores regarding its impact and effectiveness.

What we are really saying is, to get at the preacher's real identity, we must ask other questions of a more basic character. What happens when he or she preaches? Does what is done in the pulpit weld the congregation into a positive, cohesive force in and for the sake of the community? Is the preaching, for example, on Sunday morning in First Church, Hometown, USA, such that people ask themselves: What shall we do about it?—as a group, as individuals, at the desk, or store counter, or commuter train, or in the kitchen? Is there something about this preacher and his or her preaching that suggests such words as "impact," "relevance," "effectiveness," or "decision"? Was Calvin all too idealistic when he wrote, "For God wills that in the words of his witnesses his own voice should resound"?[1] What image arises in our minds when we hear the word "preacher"? Authority figures? Peddler of pious niceties? Herald of good news? Or, servant?

At this point, however, we need to ask the more basic question, What is preaching? In the opinion of this writer, few definitions of preaching improve upon that of the English layman, Bernard Manning, who said, "Preaching is the manifestation of the Incarnate Word, from the Written Word, by the Spoken Word." What do we have here? "Manifestation of the Incarnate Word"—an unveiling or a making plain of God's Word made flesh. "From the Written Word"—the substance comes from the Bible which is the record of human witness to God's many acts, particularly the supreme act of salvation in and through Christ. "By the Spoken Word"—a person speaking and communicating. And since we cannot have a manifestation without eyes to see it and ears to hear it and minds to grasp it, a listening congregation is assumed. In other words, the act of preaching in its totality and comprehensiveness might be set out before us in this way: its what-ness (a word, a message, *the* Word, good news); its who-ness (a preacher who interprets the Word, shows its relevance, and witnesses to its truth); and its where-ness (an act of worship). Moreover, the focus of all of this is people in their needs, concerns, temptations, sense of lostness, and failures.

Those lines describe the act of preaching. Its parameters are suggested by John Gross's (Book Review editor, *The New York Times*) phrase, "The which-ness of the what-ness and the where-ness of the who." But who is the preacher? Calvin talked about "the miracle by which God makes the Word of his witnesses as we find it in the Bible his own piercing Word."[2] The purpose of preaching, he held, was to lay bare and interpret the Word of God as it comes to us in the Scriptures. Farmer took this idea and put it into a succinct title for his Warrack Lectures: the preacher is "Servant of the Word" who is responsible to people. And Jenkins endorsed a similar conception when he wrote, "It is clear from Scripture that the ministry of the Church is, like that of its Lord, in the form of a servant and that it loses its meaning whenever that is forgotten."[3]

Our subsequent discussion will be an examination of "servant of the Word" in order to see its meaning for our understanding of the identity of the preacher today.

WHAT DO WE MEAN BY THE WORD?

Ours is an age bombarded by words. Ours is a highly verbal society. It is true that movies, television, mime, ballet, and so forth, have enlarged the nonverbal media of communications, but these are not an indication that there is less speaking. Communication systems are acquiring more and more new channels—medium of sight (visual arts), sound (music and other syncopated rhythm), mood (color, shades, atmosphere)—but the basic medium is words, either spoken or written. Despite some things Marshall McLuhan thought and wrote, the spoken word is with us for a while yet. In *The Presence of the Word*, Walter J. Ong of Yale wrote, "Man communicates with his whole body, yet the word is his primary medium."[1] Moreover, the word, either written or spoken, has been not only the primary vehicle of communication, but it has also been the instrument for accuracy, preservation of learning, criticism of other media, and interpretation of other attempts and methods. Whatever value other media may have, their impact and effectiveness are measured by whether through them the message "comes to speech" (Reginald Fuller's phrase). If not, the message remains elusive, subjective, impressionistic, and temporal.

Communication, we must note, is and must be always dialog-ical. This is why terms and phrases such as "encounter," "meet-ing of minds," "confrontation," "interface" are so common today. All of these suggest one presence engaging with another. Professor Ong is right in saying: "Voice conveys presence as noth-ing else does." In Shakespeare's *Hamlet*, for example, the ghost of Hamlet's father appeared at midnight before Horatio and the guards. They saw it, felt it, and were moved by fear of it, but its real presence for them must come to words. Horatio cried out: "By heaven, I charge thee speak—stay, speak, speak, I charge thee SPEAK!" "Modes of encounter," Ong continued, "are innumerable—a glance, a gesture, a touch, even an odor—but among these the spoken word is paramount."[5] Sight, sound, odor—all serve according to their capacities, but words are essential to establish communication fully. Moreover, in our "speaking-hearing" culture, the word is inseparable from action because it evokes response, creates community, initiates social-ization, and interjects the person into the mainstream of human events.

Now, preaching is not merely a matter of our words or our handling of them; it has to do with *the* Word, else it is not Chris-tian preaching. What is the difference between *the* Word and ordinary human talk? Both are instruments of communication. But while mere human words can be neutral, God's Word is never separated from the will, purpose, and action of the One who originates it.

Let us digress a bit. Whenever we examine a word analyti-cally, we talk about its derivation, connotation, and so forth. But what about "word" itself? The Greek equivalent is *logos*. For the Greeks, this word was the symbol of human activity in think-ing and reasoning and, hence, mind, spirit, and thought were involved. It had to do with the essence of things and, therefore, it was the most adequate term for that grasp of meaning by which a person saw oneself in one's place in the universe. The Greeks, however, had another word, *rhēma*, which also meant "word," but in addition *rhēma* connoted "expressed will."[6] In the Old

Testament the term for "word" was *dabar* which combines the meaning of *logos* and *rhēma*. When we analyze a word we postulate two main elements: dianoetic and dynamic. Take *dabar*, for example: from the dianoetic perspective it means "a thought, an idea, or substance." To grasp the *dabar* of anything is to have its meaning made clear or its real nature brought to light. From the dynamic perspective, every *dabar* has in it a latent power which is perceived and felt by anyone who receives the word and appropriates it to him- or herself.

Consider the case of Jeremiah in the Old Testament. The ancient Hebrew Torah was given to the priests, but the prophet was the agent of *dabar*. Jeremiah was called a prophet (1:5) who was given a word, a *dabar*, by God, a sort of inner essence (1:9) and this was embodied in his message (1:11, 12). Now the *dabar* he talked about was not merely in a dianoetic sense, but something dynamic, something to be wrestled with, something that put him under a divine constraint ("There is in my heart as it were a burning fire shut up in my bones, and I am weary with holding it in, and I cannot," 20:9). "He is inwardly aflame with the Word of [God] and will perish if he does not speak. . . . It demands to be passed on in his preaching." There is a difference to be noted, moreover, between the ordinary and the real prophet. To quote G. Kittel further, "The prophet . . . in whom is God's Word tells God's Word."[7] According to Jeremiah, that Word can be truly declared only by a person who has been broken by it and seized by it; here, in other words, was an intimation of servanthood. What is more, this *dabar* was not a static entity; it implied power (28:9, 10). It was never destined to fail; it was ever on a mission to emerge in new creations amid the old. Isaiah wrote, "So shall my word be that goes forth from my mouth; it shall not return to me empty, but it shall accomplish that which I purpose" (55:10).

When we come to the New Testament, the best-known reference to *logos* is the Prologue to John's Gospel. Linguists and biblical scholars trace the concept to Philo of Alexandria who helped unite Jewish religious ideas and those of Greek philosophy. Hence, *logos* here takes a new direction. According to Philo, *logos* was a mediating factor coming forth from God and creating a link between a remote Being and the world. In Philo's thinking, however, it was not something pinpointed in time; it was a continuous process always working, always creating, and always unfolding. But in John, and in the New Testament generally, the Word is a spoken word, spoken by God to the world at a particular point in human history. It is a revelation. It is a person who speaks God's Word to humankind. It has its own personal identity, but it points always to God who originates it. The concept here is really *dabar*, a word dianoetically, but more—a word dynamic in action. The Word here is no mere concept; it is a fuller event that took place and in which God declared God self once and for all. Christianity, then, is not a doctrine or theory proclaimed by Christ or merely a theology of an early community: it is something present in Christ's person, an event given by God with him and which he himself is.

Now, to the early prophets—Moses, Elijah, Isaiah, Jeremiah, and so on—God's Word came as a "vision" and, therefore, these men were called "see-ers" (seers). These encounters were "happenings." But words are needed to identify, explain, and record these happenings, because although something was communicated by God to the prophet through a vision, that something was communicated by the prophet to the people through words.

What, then, do we have here? God speaks and in that event or happening (because God's Word is always God's act) we have a revelation, a disclosure, a concretizing of God's will and purpose in the midst of history. Every Word from the mouth of God is creative and/or redemptive and it acts creatively and redemptively in its encounter with everything God has made. When we turn to the New Testament, the Word comes again as a happening, but this time in a Person. "The Word became flesh" (John 1:14). And when that Word appeared in Jesus, it was, first of all, eschatological, that is, the fulfillment of humanity's ageless climb to become Godlike was *here* in a person like ourselves. "The kingdom of God" was in our midst. Second, it was a reality: Jesus would never say "the Word of God came to me," as did the prophets, but "*I* say unto you . . ." Third, it was an action: God's reconciliation through judgment and love appeared in what Jesus was and did. Fourth, it was good news: the saving Word of God becoming real in a Person was something surprisingly new. It was good news; God had visited and redeemed the people. The fact of Christ was the Word of God in its fullest expression, declared once and for all time. Christ did not merely announce the Word; it was incorporated in his person; he was the great "I am." In his monograph *The Atonement*, R. W. Dale wrote: "The real truth is that while he came to preach the gospel, his chief object in coming was that there might be a gospel to preach."[8]

After the resurrection, the disciples were called to live the Christ-happening. And the New Testament is the record of their action and witness. The Book of Acts is the story of the preacher and the living Christ, both working to reconcile men and women to God. There was something of a dynamic union between them and the risen Christ. And their preaching continued to proclaim to the world what was the Word of God that came to humankind in Christ. Moreover, they would have gotten nowhere had they themselves not been a manifestation of the power of the Word of God at work. Because of what they had heard and knew and experienced, they had to preach. Indeed, there would have been no hearing and no faith without their preaching. Savonarola, the great fifteenth-century preacher and reformer, said after his own conversion to the preaching ministry, "A Word did it!" Christian preaching declared the Christ-event and for those who heard and received it, it meant having faith in Jesus.

Today the preacher's job is, as Eduard Schweizer phrased it, "to take words once spoken and make them speak again." The Scriptures must not remain as dead tablets of stone; they must become a living voice. "The written Word" is the Word of God in deep freeze. It must be unfrozen and made to speak again if it is to be heard as the living Word of God. The Christ-happening must be made present again and again through the living voice of the preacher. In commenting on the preaching of Calvin and the Reformers, T. H. L. Parker said: "Preaching is the hand-maiden of the Eternal Word which God once uttered and which was witnessed to by the words of the prophets and apostles."[9] And, as someone else said, "The voice of the sender is heard when he who was sent speaks."

Basically and simply, then, preaching is communication, but with this difference: it is the communication of the communi-cated, namely, the will and purpose of God as they are incorpo-rated in a Person and are now being worked out in history. Preaching is, in John Marsh's phrase, "the actualization of the Word." In the sermon, the Word which God spoke by historic actions is intended to come to contemporary effectiveness. This is why Heinrich Bullinger said *Praedicatio verbi Dei est verbum Dei* ("The preaching of the Word of God is the Word of God"). In other words, if our words as preachers bear faithful witness to God's Word, through them people will hear God speaking to them. Both Ernest Fuchs and Gerhard Ebeling have maintained that there must be a fresh coming-to-speech in which Jesus is heard anew. This is the miracle that occurs Sunday after Sunday when our words as preachers, strangely and mysteriously, become the Word of God. Karl Barth's point of view is similar: "The fact that sinful and erring man as such spoke the Word of God, that is the miracle of which we speak when we say the Bible is the Word of God."[10]

3
The Preacher's Identity:
Servant

SERVANT OF THE WORD

"Servant of the Word"—this is Farmer's phrase. What about "servant" as regards the preacher? Speaking of Calvin as an expository preacher, Leroy Nixon wrote, "In the pulpit he spoke not in his own name, but always and only in the name of God, whose servant he was."[1] Now, by servant here one does not mean a hired person—a flunky or "gofer"—a person who is being constantly pushed around. Certainly this is not the biblical concept. In the Bible the connotation of servant is somewhat complicated, chiefly because it has been defined or described by various writers in differing situations. There are, however, several characteristics that emerge as common factors and there are two in particular.

The first has to do with the role of the servant which we may frame from the "servant" passages in the prophecy of Isaiah. Here the servant is not just "the man for others" (which need not be anything more than a welfare worker or YMCA promoter), but is a person with God's Word for others. The Old Testament servant is not merely an avid humanitarian, but is both guardian and proclaimer of certain truths without which a person or community cannot be made whole.

Incidentally, Paul had the servant idea of the preacher in mind in 2 Cor. 4:5: "What we preach is not ourselves, but Jesus Christ as Lord, with ourselves as your servants for Jesus' sake." To digress a moment: this is a fault of so much preaching today. Women and men preach *themselves*. And this has done more to discredit preaching than most of us imagine. For this reason, critics of the pulpit are led to declare the half-truth, "The day of preaching is over." It is true that people do not flock today as they once did to Charles H. Spurgeon's tabernacle or to Brooks's Holy Trinity a century ago, but still this cynical remark conveys a lie. If you and I believe that ours is a God who speaks and if we acknowledge humanity and our world to be in a mess, then it is our business as preachers to confront a sinning world with a speaking and saving God. And one of the best ways to do this is through preaching. Preaching (that is, the right kind of preaching) is and has ever been a means of grace. Discussion groups cannot take the place of preaching, although they can be useful before or after the act of worship. Behind the dialogue, and indeed within it, there must be the Word, without which God's redeeming work cannot be completed. There can be ad hoc discussion groups, but there is no such thing as ad hoc preaching. Preaching lays upon the preacher a frightful demand; it exacts a price. Its prerequisites are basically spiritual, but they include also sweat and guts, a toll all too few today are willing to pay. Fosdick described preaching as "drenching your congregation with one's lifeblood."[2] And wherever or whenever that reality and concern are sincerely manifest, hungry sheep come to be fed.

The biblical concept of servant, however, has another and very important aspect: the manner in which it is implemented and fulfilled in and by the pulpit. This takes us back to the time of Moses and we find the first intimation of it in Exod. 32:31–32, where he offers to assume responsibility for the guilt of his own people. This idea grows gradually in thought through the Old Testament and it comes to its fullest expression in the Servant Songs of Deutero-Isaiah, especially in chapter 53. Here the servant is chosen for mission and for service. He sees in God what God wants women and men to be, and he commits himself to the realization of this ideal in human experience.

Then, in the New Testament, the way of the servant comes to its apex in the life and witness of Jesus. One has only to read the

Servant Songs in Isaiah, then the story of Jesus' baptism (Mark 1; Matt. 3:13–17), then the story of the temptation (Matt. 4:1– 11), and see thereby how Jesus appropriated into his life and mission the servant concept. At his baptism there came to him the tremendous consciousness of *who* he was; his Sonship was assured ("This is my beloved Son . . ."); but the role of Messiahship was his problem, that is, *how* this mission was to be accomplished. This is what drove him into the wilderness where for forty days he fought through a great spiritual struggle; it was the servant idea that won out. In essence, servanthood to him meant self-investment in another's moral and spiritual self-realization and fulfillment, which could add up to a cross.

What, then, does it mean for a preacher to be called a "servant of the Word"? To be servant of the Word the preacher so gives herself or himself to others that the creative and redemptive Word in and through the preacher might be formed in others. This is what Paul meant when he said, "My little children, with whom I am again in travail until Christ be formed in you" (Gal. 4:19). Think of the responsibility. The demand. The precedent that is set. As preachers it asks you and me so to give ourselves to others that the Christ in us might be formed in them.

THE NEED FOR PERSONAL WITNESS

What will be the character of the preacher and of the preaching that takes the servant of the Word concept and demand seriously?

As servant of the Word, the preacher as a person is more clearly identified with the essence of Christian preaching. The preacher has suffered always from the traditional jibe leveled at all Christians: the chasm between what we say and what we are. Usually it is expressed in the aphorism attributed to Emerson: "What you are speaks so loudly I cannot hear a word you say." Some years ago the Literary Supplement of *The London Times* printed an article entitled "The Empty Pews," by an able and astute English layman, Charles Morgan. In it he gave a very pointed appraisal of the nature and quality of English preaching, and what he said can be applied easily to America. He made three judgments:

Sermons are disappointing, not because they are too long, but because they are too scanty. They do not strike deeply enough. Remember in Ibsen's play *Peer Gynt* how Peer, returning from the funeral of a man of a wretched reputation and over whom the preacher had delivered a soft and unctuous eulogy, remarked: "There was nothing in it to make you feel uneasy."

As some preachers mount the pulpit, they seem to put aside the authority of their calling. They are so anxious not to appear as "parsons" that they avoid even a distinctively Christian approach to their subject and discuss it as if they were merchants or politicians. Some people in the pews may say "Our preacher is so humble." But such a pulpit posture repels more than attracts.

Lay people are never claimed by a preacher who talks down to them. If the preacher's argument is in effect a "lay" argument, that is, the kind that may be heard in any service club or read in any newspaper, the preacher is teaching women and men what they do not go to church to learn. They go to church to worship, to hear their faith expounded, and to learn how Christian teaching bears upon their daily life, and these from preachers who, fearlessly and without compromise, refer their subject to the basic truths of Christianity.

These judgments are disturbing, but much more so when we read Bishop William A. Quale's famous prescription regarding preaching and the preacher: "Preaching is the art of making a sermon and delivering it? Why, no, that's not preaching! Preaching is the art of making a preacher and delivering that. Preaching is the outrush of the soul in speech. Therefore the elemental business in preaching is not with preaching, but with the preacher. . . . What, then, in the light of this, is the task of the preacher? Mainly this: the amassing of a great soul so as to have something worthwhile to give; the sermon is the preacher up to date."[3]

This quotation suggests that maybe too much of our preaching has been a matter of proclaiming and little more. *Webster's Dictionary* gives a plausible definition of preaching—"to exhort in a tedious and tiresome manner." Preaching of this kind has an "at-ness" with no "together-ness." And, as such, it is merely monological. Reuel Howe has commented, "The word spoken in a monologue is a concluding word. The word spoken in dialogue is a beginning."[1] One of the biblical terms for preacher is "herald." The idea is that she or he is one who proclaims. But proclamation is not sufficient in itself. That would be preaching without the preacher. Christian preaching in the Acts of the Apostles was not proclamation alone; it was proclamation *and* witness. The central substance of their preaching was the kerygma: the publication of certain facts about the life and death of Jesus Christ, and chiefly his resurrection. But an interesting and significant item is frequently overlooked: in most of the references in Acts to the preaching of the apostles, the common fact was not only the resurrection, there was another—this event was certified to by many witnesses (Acts 2:32; 3:15; 10:40–41; 31:30–31). Their proclamation, then, was not merely imparting certain information; it was *witness* in which the person testifying was completely involved. The preacher and the preaching had a unique identification when the substance of the proclamation was witnessed to in all honesty by the person who proclaimed.

This spells out some important counsel for preaching and the preacher in our time. Never have preachers faced a more inhospitable world than they do today. An unfavorable climate has been created, not merely by human sin (if such a term has significance any longer), but also by those institutions which should be the preacher's allies. Many universities, colleges, and other centers of learning have been engaged in telling generations of students—as Walter Cronkite once remarked— "how to make a fast buck rather than how to find life's meaning." Many preachers have held up before their people and have glamorized the "success image" rather than declaring and witnessing to the New Testament model of being among women and men "as one who serves." This is why the new generation has been inclined to have none of us. Listen to their vocabulary: "integrity," "honesty," "authenticity," "turn us on," "ethical involvement," and the like. Can the Christian pulpit go on "shoring up" the value structure of the prevailing culture of the hour? No preacher can continue to face this age with a small message. Neither can one declare a big message which one has no right to speak. And the latter is assured and guaranteed only when the proclamation of the pulpit (its what-ness) is underscored by the preacher's witness (the why-ness of it all).

No preacher should presume today, therefore, to invent the substance of her or his message or to hand out to the people something created according to the preacher's own convenience. There must be evidence that the preacher first *received* it and has been *involved* in it. Barth once used three phrases to describe the work of the preacher from the moment she or he chooses a text to the time of delivery in or from the pulpit: speak after (i.e., do your exegetical work first and find out what the text says), speak with (i.e., carry on your own dialogue with the text), and speak to (i.e., be sure the text speaks *through* the preacher to the world).[5] This is the crucial moment: when the Word speaks through the preacher to the human problem and with the resounding *I know* of the servant witness, that Word comes to what Marsh called "contemporaneous effectiveness." Calvin called the Bible "the organ of a living will." And John Wycliffe declared that "his God-given task was to make the Bible available to the man in the street." To this breed of preacher, the world of needy souls will listen, for they sense that the preacher has wrestled with something or Someone outside and beyond self and, therefore, has gotten a new slant on life's meaning, has handled the very stuff of people's everyday problems, and from the very depths of their own experience says to the congregation, "This is the way, walk in it" (Isa. 30:21).

IDENTIFICATION WITH THE PEOPLE

As servant of the Word the preacher is more effectively involved with the congregation. Martin Buber's "I-thou" concept became in theological circles a slogan for spiritual encounter. It shares a common familiarity with Rudolph Otto's descriptive phrase for God as the "wholly other." These phrases are merely attempts to suggest the qualitative difference between God and humankind. But heresy crept in and has tried to make us believe that between God and God's creatures there was "a great gulf fixed." And the new breed, inside and outside the church, has used this concept for deploring the cleavage between divine and human, clergy and laity, pulpit and pew, established church and secular community, and other dichotomies ad infinitum. Methods are being invented and tried to erase this division. For example, bridges between pulpit and pew are being suggested and attempted: cell groups, lay discussions before and after the sermon, discarding of the clerical collar, less emphasis upon ministry as an order. The monological character of the sermon has been called into question. New forms of communication have been tried: panels, dialogues, and the like. Much of this, however, has been precipitated by a misunderstanding of the relationship between pulpit and pew. Could it be possible that the concept of the preacher as servant would remedy some of these so-called abuses?

Certain obvious things can be done and done rather easily: Consider the preacher's vocabulary. Why do some preachers hang on to the language of Canaan? Or the thought concepts and idioms of the Victorian age? So many are addicts to the "parsonic phrase"—never do they use "said" but "voiced," nothing is "described" but "depicted," no one has simply "seen" but "viewed," and most irksome of all are verb formations such as "to fellowship," "to pastor," "to author." Calvin defined language as the key to "social intercourse." Why, then, is the pulpit so slow to select the usable idioms of our day?

The preacher may magnify one area of the ministry at the expense of all the others. Ours must be a balanced witness and it must be done through counseling, visitation, teaching, worship, and preaching. Wholeness of ministry results when each of these informs and supports the others. As servant of the Word, however, the preacher is involved more effectively with her or his people than at any other time or place. Theodore Ferris once remarked: "When my preaching runs dry, I know it is time to get back to my Bible and my people."[6]

What should happen, then, when the servant of the Word preaches to a congregation on Sunday morning? What must the enterprise be like so that the Christ in the preacher is formed in them?

An audience must be made into a congregation. On Sunday morning, the preacher stands before several hundred disparate individuals who must be welded into a unit. One has less and less enthusiasm for the term "body," because in these days it is associated more with corporations, establishments, and other decision-making groups. Far more preferable is the word "organism." As an organism a congregation is a company of women and men who have caught the Christlike spirit in the act of worship and who then carry its contagion out into the life of society. To quote Forsyth again, "You are to preach the Gospel to the Church so that with the Church you will bring the Gospel to the world."[7] There are two major differences between a lecture in a secular situation and preaching in an act of worship to a congregation: (1) Intention—whenever any speech is delivered, communication takes place and some response or feedback is elicited. In preaching, the response must always be a desired response. (2) Operation—whenever any speech is delivered, the speaker uses words as the means of entering into the life and consciousness of the hearers. With preaching, the difference is in the content of those words and the speaker's relation to it. As servant of the Word, she or he declares a fact: God is in action (John 3:16) and no one within hearing can be indifferent to it. The

preacher puts the language of today at the disposal of the living
Christ and draws implications for the everyday life of the hearers. But, at the same time, one must be oneself and deny oneself.
The preacher must show people what this Word has done to her-
or himself and at the same time deny self by pointing her or his
people beyond her- or himself. As servants of the Word the
preacher's preaching must become an actualization of the Word.
This is what John Wesley meant when, after preaching to an
open-air crowd, he commented: "I gave them Christ." John
Knox also implied this when he referred to that preaching in
which the event is in a real sense "recurring." Or Calvin's significant remark, "The preaching of the Gospel is like a descent that
God makes to come to seek us."[8] In every sermon God ought to
come to us in Jesus Christ. And in our response to it the church as
an organism is constituted and nourished.

The congregation must be pointed toward action. What we
do on Sunday morning is not so much a service of worship as it is
an act of worship whose outlet or consequence is service. In this
ceremonial the preacher tells and witnesses to what it means to
be a Christian, what it means to be "in Christ." For this the
preacher must be "bilingual" (Krister Stendahl's phrase), that is,
she or he must show how the experiences of Christ in the first
century are and can be reenacted in the experiences of women
and men today. For some hearers, it will come as a word of judgment; for others, an awakened conscience; for still others, a time
to rejoice and to resolve to live meaning into the Word of the
gospel. Whatever the response—whether it be yea or nay—a
meaningful encounter has occurred; the kingdom has impinged
upon some of them and a new day for them has begun. This is the
great moment for the servant of the Word, the moment when, as
Joseph Sittler said, "God's deed becomes a possibility for man's
need."[9] Here the involvement of the preacher with the congregation becomes real and effective; here is where the action really
begins. Now the servant's word and witness come full circle and
the people ask, "What will you have us to do?"

Many years ago, Robert Norwood, then rector of St. Bartholo-
mew's Church, New York City, was celebrating the twenty-fifth
anniversary of his ordination, and he told his congregation a
story. When he was a young man, just ordained, his father
invited him to preach in his pulpit in a little parish called Hub-
bards on the southeast coastline of the province of Nova Scotia.
Young Robert considered it a great opportunity to be asked to
preach in his father's pulpit and before his home congregation.
During the week he worked intensely and feverishly on the sermon and loaded it with glowing phrases and purple passages.
Sunday came and Robert preached. On the way home, however,
he was disturbed that his father made no mention whatsoever of
the sermon. And Robert, in his boyish conceit, concluded,
"Well, he's so overwhelmed by this young Chrysostom that he
can't find words to express his appreciation." Nothing was said
the rest of the day. But, then, late in the day as they sat together
before the fireplace in his study, the old man said in an indirect
connection, "There are two ways to preach: one way is to stand
in front of the Cross and magnify yourself; the other is to lift up
the Cross and keep yourself out of sight."

It is this point of view (to use Jenkins's words) "that enables the
preacher to accomplish that bringing of his mind into 'the form
of a servant,' that bringing of every thought 'into the captivity of
Christ' which enables him [her] to be the vehicle of God's true
and living Word."[10]

4
The Word in the Sermon

If being a servant of the Word becomes the spiritual and vocational faculty of the preacher, what influence does it have upon the making of the sermon in the preacher's long-range approach to this responsibility? What influence does it have in the actual execution of the sermon in its successive stages of completion?

PRELIMINARY CONCERNS

A viable theology of the Bible is basic. Every preacher must settle this question in his or her mind early upon assuming the ministry of preaching. True, it may change somewhat or even radically through the years as the preacher makes the Bible the close companion of daily meditation and study and as new vistas of the nature of the Bible as revelation are encountered and appropriated. Nevertheless, in order to be a servant of the Word, every preacher must reckon with the elementary question: What is the Bible to me? Among the more useful monographs to serve any preacher toward a mature personal verdict: *Preface to Bible Study*, by Alan Richardson (London: SCM Press, 1943); *The Bible To-day*, by C. H. Dodd (New York: Macmillan Co., 1947); *The Bible Speaks to You*, by Robert McA. Brown (Philadelphia: Westminster Press, 1955); *The Interpretation of Scripture*, by James D. Smart (Philadelphia: Westminster Press, 1961); *Theology of the Old Testament*, by W. Eichrodt (Philadelphia: Westminster Press, 1961); *Old Testament Theology*, by G. von Rad (Edinburgh and London: Oliver & Boyd, 1963); *An Introduction to New Testament Thought*, by F. C. Grant (Nashville: Abingdon-Cokesbury Press, 1950); *New Testament Theology*, by Ethelbert Stauffer (London: SCM Press, 1955); and *Biblical Theology, Contemporary,* by Krister Stendahl (Nashville: Abingdon Press, 1962)—to name merely a few.

The line of action of the Bible in the sermon must be carefully considered. In preaching, the Bible is both source and resource. It is the source when in one's reading, meditation, or exegetical analysis and probing, a word concept or seminal idea leaps out of the Scripture and speaks its message directly. This, on this critical occasion, is the Word of God to and for the preacher and the sermon takes its genesis from it. Moreover, the sermon that takes its origin from an experience such as this is most likely to be unique with you, to bear the imprint and fruit of a deeper inspiration, and have a message for the congregation that differs from commonplace moralisms and self-help aphorisms.

The Bible is also a resource for preaching. When a human problem is localized in the community, or a moral issue is hurting the congregation, or a crisis has disturbed the national conscience, the people are inclined to turn to the pulpit for a word that is more satisfying and stabilizing than the average advice to "remain calm." They ask rather pointedly, "Is there any word from the Lord?" The preacher then turns to the Bible and searches for an answer. Caution must be taken in this latter strategy, however, lest the preacher's own personal opinion or cast of mind color the Word from the Bible and make the sermon an exercise in eisegesis.

Every sermon must be biblically contextual as well as contextually liturgical. Initially the sermon rises within the context of biblical revelation. The preacher's understanding of and commitment to this reality create an unseen companion as the sermon is crafted. It must always be present as a silent influence and sustaining inspiration, giving direction and purpose from the moment of the inception of the homiletical idea to the preacher's witness to it in the pulpit.

Another very important context is the one in which the original writer of the passage of Scripture wrote or spoke. By way of

sermonic preparation the preacher must answer the five Ws—
who said it? when was it said? where was it said? what actually
was said? why? An adequate grasp of the meaning of the text
from these queries safeguards any preacher from eisegetical handling of the original message. Schweizer's maxim is appropriate
here for every preacher, "Exegesis tells us what the writer said;
hermeneutics informs us as to what the writer meant."

One must not overlook the liturgical context, that is, the act of
worship in which the particular sermon is given. The contents of
the service include the various and traditional ingredients, all of
which come from the Bible and constitute the act of worship:
readings, prayers, hymns, sermon, sacraments, and so forth.
These compose the liturgy in which the sermon has its functional
place. This act, however, is not and must not be merely a mixed
bag, a random sequence of things people say and do in church.
The nature and intention of the Word and the way it operates in
worship gives to the service its shape, its direction, and above all,
its meaning. Every preacher who claims to be a servant of the
Word should not allow the enterprise over which he or she pre-
sides to continue to neglect the role that Word should play in
shaping the order of Sunday worship, the handling of the sacraments, the architectural form of the sanctuary, and the whole
complexion of the Christian education program of the people. It
is puzzling to observe how many ministers and congregations
who clamor for preaching with biblical and theological orientation are satisfied to take part weekly in services that are a jumble
of ill-sorted items entirely devoid of the theological rationale
that being servants of the Word demands.

Every preacher should read at least one good book each year
on preaching and worship. Andrew W. Blackmood used to
advise his students to avoid "ephemeral stuff." The contemporary market is glutted with them. Mail-order flyers advertise
"Powerful Preaching in Six Easy Lessons" or "Sermon Starters
for Harried Preachers." Choices must be made discriminately;
however, one's favorite modern homilist is always acceptable

and useful as long as, every two years, the preacher reads Phillips Brooks, *Lectures on Preaching*, and Peter T. Forsyth, *Positive Preaching and the Modern Mind*. Brooks admirably weds preaching and pastoral work; Forsyth puts preaching and worship into theological perspective with unrivaled competence.

PREPARATORY STEPS

There are eight steps that spell out a useful procedure in crafting the sermon. These are not intended to be mechanically separate units; rather, they are implementations of a method of interpreting the Word, showing its relevance, and instructing a congregation. The overall operation and procedure must be underscored by prayer, study, sweat, and guts.

Accumulation of information. What will you preach on next Sunday? Lectionary preaching is either assumed or required by some denominations. It is increasingly becoming a practice among other denominations which traditionally had avoided such systems. Whatever schema is employed, however, every preacher ought to adhere to a system of planned preaching. The festivals of the Christian year will claim initial priority, then the national and civic observances, and in-between there are opportunities for sermon series which are excellent vehicles for the preacher to reach the people's needs as their teacher. For some, slavish adherence to the lectionary limits outreaches of the imagination, whereas, for others, the lectionary challenges and develops perceptive excursions into areas and about themes easily neglected.

Where will you get your materials? Basically the Bible will be your staple. In addition to a one-volume biblical commentary for handy reference, the preacher's shelves should have two commentaries—one exegetical and one expositional—on each book of the Bible. Auxiliary resources will be general reading, observations of and reflections upon life, and the choice of one major congenial theologian whose writings challenge your own ideas and who can become your companion for decades. Only by such a disciplined study program will a preacher's thinking retain a cutting edge.

Equally important is the amassing and conserving of a subsoil of ideas upon which to draw and to which one must add constantly. This assumes an adequate and efficient filing system. Any preacher neglects such at his or her own peril. Collecting ideas, quotations, illustrations, and so on, in a carefully card-indexed system is imperative; it is the antidote to the disease of dull preaching and a very early warning to the laggard who all too soon finds himself or herself "preached out." The discipline such an enterprise requires is not always embraced by busy preachers, but without it their "busy-ness" is tantamount to a recipe for pulpit dullness or even failure.

Brood over the text. It might be a lectionary choice or a text with an arresting idea rising with a challenging voice during your morning devotions and saying "Preach on me." The procedure begins with the clearing of your desk of all distracting items: reminders of things to do, odd pieces of unfinished work, names of persons to be telephoned, periodicals, and any other minutiae associated with the daily round. Read the Scripture passage in every translation available on your reference shelf (KJV, RSV, NEB, JB, TEV, NIV, etc.). If you are proficient in Hebrew or Greek, make your own translation. These things ended, begin your initial "brooding" period. A clean sheet of paper or notepad is taken and designated "Worksheet 1." What is this pericope of Scripture saying to you? Brainstorm for maybe an hour or two, jotting down everything your mind suggests. Wring your brain dry. The result will be a collage of ideas: fragments of thought, recollections of things read or seen in past experiences, insights into current issues and problems, echoes of sermons once heard or read, snatches of poetry and hymns, and so on. What is the advantage of all this? It is your firsthand reflections upon the text and what it calls forth from the totality of your human learning and experience. It is the fruit of your initial encounter with the text. Hence, it will bring the marks of

your own originality to the emerging sermon and will put upon
the final product the stamp of your own mind and person.

With this stage completed, you will now move to the commentaries. Many preachers, incidentally, consult the commentaries
first, which is a mistake. This allows the commentary to influence the direction of your thinking and, therefore, cancels out
your own originality, the first-time-ness of your own thought.
Commentaries are necessary as correctives of and as contribu-
tors to your ideas once your primary research has been done.
With them in hand, take a fresh page, "Worksheet 2." The focus
is now upon context: the 5 Ws—*who, what, when, where,* and
why. All relevant notations are jotted down and other useful
ideas are included.

Place the first and second worksheets before you and *begin
another brooding session.* This is critically important. Unfortunately, with many preachers it is frequently underdone. Brooding must not be hurried or in any way interrupted or
shortchanged. Suddenly—sometimes early, sometimes late—
there comes the moment of illumination, the aha! experience.
Out of the collage of notations, an idea leaps at you, arresting
you, and becomes the Word of God to and for you, the fruit of
your prayerful insight into truth in your solitary trust with Scripture. Immediately start "Worksheet 3" and at the top of the page
state in one succinct sentence this central idea which will be the
integrating theme of the sermon and the pivotal point around
which your message will take its shape.

All the foregoing achieved, the next step is *relevance.* What is
the point of immediacy of this Word among your people? Where
does this idea hit whom? To what situation in your parish does it
speak a word of judgment or reconciliation? Here your pastoral
acumen must come into play. And you must use your pastoral
awareness and sensitivity, for as Brooks declared, "A minister
who is a preacher and not a pastor becomes remote; a minister
who is a pastor and not a preacher becomes petty."[1]

The message and pastoral situation (it can be personal,

national, or generally human) must now be brought into *focus*.
If the basis of the sermon is a Scripture passage, maybe the central idea is conveyed strikingly in and through one particular
text. The focus is achieved by bringing that text and the human
situation together and hammering out a succinct topic. A good
topic must be arresting, evoke human interest and concern, and
have in it essentially an overtone of the Christian religion. With
this done, it is time now to decide on your purpose. What is to be
the objective of this sermon? As Fosdick so well said and prac-
ticed: "My silent prayer each Sunday morning before the sermon
started was: 'O God, some one person here needs what I am
going to say. Help me to reach him.'"[2]

It is time to brood again. The sermon is actually the extension
of the central idea. Return to the first and second worksheets and
with topic, text, and purpose in mind select from them the major
ideas to be the main developmental thoughts of the sermon. The
introduction is identified when you ask yourself, how shall I
break in upon my congregation's attention? This material must
be engaging, provocative, and contemporary. Or, as George
Buttrick put it in an informal critique, "Do not reach the second
paragraph of your sermon without convincing the persons in the
pews that what you are talking about is their concern." As the
outline of the sermon takes shape, you must consider logic (does
this make sense?), psychology (does it lift the hearers to climactic
peaks of feeling and thought?), will (does it lead to a decision or a
verdict in favor of the essentials of Christian faith and belief?).

With this full outline before you (Worksheet 3), you must
address the message to life. Ask yourself: Is this merely theory?
An essay? Or is it a living organism? What will this sermon do
this Sunday morning within the context of the service of worship? The outline must be fleshed out now with human illustrations, quotable opinions (biblical and secular), the experiences
of named religious authorities, your own witness from personal
encounters through the years. Care must be taken to keep the
outline dominant and clear so that, as Brooks reminded us, the

people will be able to follow your thinking and remember the sermon when they leave.

The final step in crafting the sermon is to *write it out in full*. Careful writing has certain built-in safeguards and benefits. The discipline of writing helps ideas to be well expressed. It keeps the preacher from becoming sloppy in the way sentences are shaped and said. In good writing you are more apt to say what you mean. With some preachers it provides necessary terminal facilities; they are more inclined thereby to stop when they end. Fosdick's observation is a warning to all pulpiteers: "As I have watched preachers who do not write, I have seen the almost inevitable result: monotonous style, limited vocabulary with few synonyms, repetitious ruts of thought, and finally a quick change of pastorate."[3]

EXAMPLES
Pericope: John 15:1-11

Worksheet 1

(The following is a sheet of the results of brooding initially upon the Scripture passage. The pattern is fragmentary, but it reflects the preacher's firsthand thinking after reading the passage in various translations. Such establishes the imprint upon the emerging sermon of one person's own originality. Unconsciously and uncannily it will influence the whole sermon.)

Note here that Jesus is the vine; God is the vinedresser; and we are the branches. The vinedresser superintends the whole operation: planting, pruning, and the like. The aim is healthy growth. The branches must get the best sustenance. Constant input guarantees output (i.e., abundant harvest). Note an emphasis upon the essential connection between vine and branch. The energy of the vine is shared with the branch. An analogy is drawn here with the personal relationship between Christ and his followers. The key or secret of it is abide in him. What is the real nature or meaning of "abide"? How? Why? Also, this is the key to fruitfulness. Absence of this connection means a fruitless life; no meaning. Verse 7 indicates it is a two-way enterprise: "Abide in me and my words abide in you." What is the meaning of "Father glorified"? Consult commentaries here. Essence of this connection or relationship is love. Originates with the Father; works through the Son. Loving God and keeping God's commandments are closely related, two sides of one coin. The end of these lessons is appropriating Christ's joy and bringing our own joy to fulfillment. The fruitful life is a common concept in Scripture and it is always linked with service. A problem is pointed up here: the incomplete life, one with no purpose, no direction, no benefit to others. One life touches another. Unimpaired connection guarantees fulfillment. Often human potential is wasted. Absence of wholeness. Lack of balance in growth and development. Fruitful life is never a passive condition. Takes positive effort, but always with God's help. May be costly. Not private. Many branches: all connected and intertwined (social implications).

Worksheet 2

The Greek text of the passage is very simple. There are no textual problems. It falls easily into five divisions: vv. 1–2; 3–6; 7–8; 9–10; 11.

Commentaries: *The Mission and Message of Jesus*, by H. D. A. Major, T. W. Manson, and C. J. Wright (New York: E. P. Dutton & Co., 1938); *The Expositor's Greek Testament: St. John*, ed. W. R. Nicoll, vol. 1 (Grand Rapids: Wm. B. Eerdmans, 1967); *The Daily Study Bible: Gospel of John*, by William Barclay, vol. 1 (Philadelphia: Westminster Press, 1956); *The Layman's Bible Commentary: John*, by F. V. Filson, vol. 19 (Richmond: John Knox Press, 1963); *The Gospel according to St. John*, by Rudolf Schnackenburg, vol. 3 (New York: Herder & Herder, 1982); and *The Gospel according to John*, by Raymond E. Brown (Garden City, N.Y.: Doubleday & Co., 1970).

Other comments from files:

"The key to John 14 is peace; the key to John 15 is fruitfulness."

Personal relationship with God through Christ is the mandate. Fruit is the symbol of life's fullest expression: its fulfillment. Human obedience is the condition of all true fellowship (Major, Manson, and Wright).

"Man can only come to himself by an intimate alliance with Christ." "Christ declares his Gospel through witnesses; therefore he has need of the branches." The branch severed from the vine means paralysis and death. But it means also an impoverished vine. The healthy branch is a vehicle for the expression of the vine. Paul said, "I live, yet not I, but Christ liveth in me" (Jowett).

"When a person has found what God means and is, that person knows joy at its best" (Frederick Meek, one-time minister of Old South Congregational Church, Boston).

"It means to have such a grasp of Christ's words, to allow his insight and wisdom to sink so deep into us that everything we think and say and do is colored by them. It does not mean 'swooning back in the arms of Jesus,' but letting the strong, realistic, God-centered thoughts of Jesus correct and guide our thought" (W. B. J. Martin, one-time columnist for *The Presbyterian Outlook*).

For further ideas and illustrative materials, see *The Expository Times* (annual index of texts) and *The Speaker's Bible*, ed. James Hastings (Grand Rapids: Baker Book House, 1963), has eight pages of homiletical commentary on this text.

Worksheet 3

Central Idea: There is one source of creative spiritual life among people; it comes from God to them through Christ. To be whole persons, therefore, we must become and continue as branches of the true vine.

Point of Immediacy: Think and brood over the passage and research materials and at the same time consider your people. What has this Scripture to say to what condition among us? Maybe life's lack of real fruitfulness; but more likely life's incompleteness. A contemporary congregation may not be inclined toward excitement over being fruitful, but most men and women are concerned with fulfillment.

Text: In order to sharpen the sermon's focus, v. 5 is useful: "For apart from me you can do nothing."

Topic: In order to bring text and central idea together into a succinct topic, this one sounds a positive note: "Life Can Be Complete." This disposes of any notion of the negative which "incomplete" and "unfruitful" suggest as concepts.

Strategy: Keep underlining the contrast between how incomplete and unfulfilled we are versus how we can become complete.

Outline:

Introduction: How incomplete we are

    I. Cite an apt quotation or a human illustration in order to give the problem what Shakespeare called "a local habitation and a name." A branch on the ground, separated from the vine, has
       A. No purpose
       B. No vitality
       C. No useful end

   II. Draw a parallel
       A. The one-sided life; lack of wholeness
       B. Advances in science without moral improvement
       C. Stores of knowledge, but no philosophy of life

  III. Emil Brunner: "Our progress in knowledge is not accompanied by a corresponding progress of moral forces"

How can we become complete? Certain principles to instruct us are in this passage from John.

I. Identify yourself with the person and company of Jesus (become a branch of the true vine). People ask *how?*
    A. Know about Christ from the New Testament (many people do not know even the rudiments of the life story of Jesus)
    B. Know Christ from his company in your prayers and devotions
    C. Nourish this relationship by worship in and with the fellowship of the church (the N.T. knows nothing of a solitary Christian)
    D. Practice this connection by joining other people in good causes (outreach of our human concern)

II. Be obedient to the claims of this new fellowship
    A. Purging and pruning are necessary to keep the vines in repair and healthy
    B. This process costs something: discipline, investment of time and care
    C. Every friendship lays a claim upon any one of us
    D. Quality and durability of a friendship depend upon how much we put into it

III. If conditions A and B are fulfilled, God assures us that our life will become complete and we shall have joy in its realization
    A. God always underwrites what God promises
    B. God's love is on deposit for those qualified to draw upon it
    C. Without this resource we can do nothing; with it we can reach complete realization of our human and spiritual potential
    D. This is the source of inner joy and satisfaction, that is, eternal life

Pericope: Psalm 103

Worksheet 1

One of the finest declarations of praise in the Book of Psalms, indeed in the Old Testament. Psalms: hymnbook of Hebrew worship. Hence, this psalm may comprise segments of traditional hymns. Focus is God but psalmist dwells not only upon God's nature and attributes, but describes in depth his own spiritual experience and the effects of his apprehension of God. God is such that the psalmist is eager to open his life to God and this openness is a byproduct of genuine thanksgiving. Psalm is a celebration of the wonderful grace of God in dealings with humankind. Nature of God and nature of humankind are contrasted; only hope for the latter lies in the concern of the former for us. Here we see the biblical notion or concept of thanksgiving as contrasted with our superficial "Thank you" and "How much more do we get?" Real thanksgiving includes faith, and faith involves decision; our gratitude is genuine only insofar as we fulfill the conditions of faith. By fulfilling these conditions we know God better. Scottish Psalter has made many psalms singable by paraphrasing them in English verse; for example, "O Thou, my soul, bless God the Lord." Also, anthem: "Bless thou the Lord" (arranged by Ippolitoff-Ivanoff).

Psalms provoke us to think of our human situation. Dearth of gratitude today. Lost note in much of our worship. Much thanksgiving is unreal. National Thanksgiving Day has no real religious focus; confused with superficial Americanism. Too late in autumn: too quick a shift from Thanksgiving to Advent. If Thanksgiving is response—to what? to whom? The eclipse of genuine thanksgiving is created partly by the contemporary eclipse of human wonder and reverence. "Amazing Grace" does not excite our wondering response or gratitude. Thanksgiving involves offering, and offering implies recognition of and obedience to a will not our own. If Thanksgiving is contained in merely a secular dimension, it becomes a cliché or pointless routine. The biblical idea of thanksgiving is dialogical: God supplies grace and we respond, but response may be more than a blasé "Thank ye." Our whole being is involved and claimed; only thereby can our thanksgiving have worthwhile effect.

Worksheet 2

The psalm falls into six thematic segments: vv. 1–2; 3–5; 6–13; 14–16; 17–18; and 19–22.

Commentaries: *The Psalms*, by Artur Weiser (Philadelphia: Westminster Press, 1962); *The Psalms*, by Lawrence Toombs (Nashville: Abingdon Press, 1971); *Preaching on the Books of the Old Testament*, by Dwight E. Stevenson (New York: Harper & Row, 1961) and *In the Biblical Preacher's Workshop*, also by Stevenson (New York: Harper & Row, 1967); and *Preaching from the Psalms*, by Kyle M. Yates (New York: Harper & Brothers, 1948).

General character of the psalm: three elements—a call to praise; a statement of motive or reason for praise; a renewed summons to praise. God is praised, not so much for what God gives us, but for what God is and what by virtue of God's nature God does (Toombs). Weiser: "This psalm is one of the finest blossoms on the tree of biblical faith."

Verses 1–2: The psalmist directs the call to himself; he yearns to meet God face to face and to open his life to God's presence. His appeal is to the *whole person:* "all that is within me." He feels a sense of awe in God's presence, yet he remembers God's personal benefits toward his own self. In this way sublimity and intimacy meet (God is far removed, yet God cares for us). This is not an antithesis: it is two facets of the same reality. Verses 1–2 are a call to bless the Lord and the psalmist directs it to himself.

Verses 3–5: Here is the psalmist's personal experience of the grace of God. His response to God opens up glimpses of what God is and does. He names negative conditions into which God enters (sin, disease, death, etc.) and transforms or removes altogether. He puts sin first: the most serious obstacle to nearness to

God. Result: confidence; fulfillment; surrounded by God's love; and new vitality. (New Testament concept is "born again.")

Verses 6–13: The psalmist catalogues experiences of God in his own life and that of the world. He projects a view and comprehension of God's care in the human story, especially for Israel. Here he sees God's righteousness and justice in action in history. The human tendency (vv. 9–10) is to try to set God into the dimensions of the way we live, act, and think. God's grace, however, is greater than we are; indeed the psalmist is overwhelmed at the magnificence of the eternal favor and concern.

Verses 14–18: God knows we are dust. But God grants to us the opportunity and blessing of sharing in God's grace. There is, however, a condition: "to keep his covenant" (vv. 17, 18).

Verses 19–22: This is a closing hymn. Unlimited dimensions of praise are here: time, space, and all constricting barriers fall. God is enthroned and the psalmist calls on the whole heavenly host to join him in praise (cf. Isa. 6:1–8; Ps. 19:1ff.).

Worksheet 3

Central Idea: Thanksgiving is real and effective only when it is a celebration of life, life redeemed by God's grace and nourished by our constant response to the claim of God's will.

Point of Immediacy: The message is intended to improve the average person's poor understanding of the nature of real thanksgiving. By exploring its meaning biblically and in depth, the sermon can be a learning experience for the congregation, with prophetic and informative overtones.

Topic: "Bringing God into Thanksgiving."

Text: Psalm 103:1.

Purpose: Mainly teaching. A definition of "thanksgiving" with moral and spiritual implications that enter the whole of life.

Sermonic Sample

Above a bed in an English hospital a bronze tablet bears these words: "This bed has been endowed by the savings of a poor man who is grateful for an unexpected recovery."

Three thousand years ago, on a dry and sandy hillside, the prophet Samuel set up a stone to celebrate the victory of Israel over the Philistines. Travelers on the road from Mizpah to Shen would see this memorial which he called "Ebenezer," meaning "the stone of help." Centuries later the hymn writer Robert Robinson caught this idea when he wrote:

> Here I raise my Ebenezer;
> Hither by thy help I'm come;
> And I hope, by thy good pleasure,
> Safely to arrive at home.

These are what we might call unique expressions of human gratitude. They illustrate those special moments when, in view of some great blessing—a deliverance, an act of mercy, or even a fresh opportunity—the feelings of a human heart welled up in praise and thankfulness, and by means of a memento have had it celebrated before the eyes of every generation following it.

But, as you and I well know, life does not consist of mountain-peak experiences alone. What about the grateful heart in "the trivial round, the common task"? An answer may be devious or difficult to come by, especially in our present confusion between rights and privileges, between mercies unmerited and achievements dearly earned. Yet it is just in this common, workaday world that the distinction between the grateful and the ungrateful is most likely to appear. It is comparatively easy on the crest of a wave of national enthusiasm to sing with the crowd "Thanks be to God" or "Alleluia," but is the situation not different when we are involved in the daily grind of colorless responsibilities in our own tiny world? Down there we discover one of the peculiar and indeed damaging characteristics of our affluent age: the alarming absence of the spirit of common gratitude.

It is not easy to find reasons for this condition, yet the evidence is disturbingly real: none of us can name many people today who are consistently grateful. Indeed, one of America's gifted preachers, upon his retirement, confided to a friend that the most widespread human fault in the average American community was sheer ingratitude.

This does not mean, however, that in these modern times we have ceased altogether to try. The annual presidential proclamation setting aside the fourth Thursday in November as a day of national thanksgiving indicates at least that we are willing to go on record as a grateful people. What we need is actually a deeper interpretation of this festive day so that those who are inclined to revel proudly and only in their self-sufficiency might catch that new sense of wonder at the eternal Goodness, both appropriate and necessary to an adequate observance of the day.

Besides this general apathy toward thanksgiving, which certainly we have in common—although with lesser reason—with other times and peoples, what ought really to create greater alarm is the way in which many otherwise levelheaded citizens treat thanksgiving with almost a smile of contempt. In certain circles in modern America it is almost impolite to indicate that you are content, that you rejoice in a stable home life in a law-abiding community, or that you believe there is still some untold mystery to our existence that makes you stand in wonder about it. To talk aloud in this way invites the possibility of being branded a reactionary, or even a fascist, and certainly as being destitute of any semblance of the critical spirit. Some of these people may tolerate a big splurge for the sake of the Thanksgiving holiday on November 23, but the rest of the year, in their two-dimensional world of reach and take, they feel there are few benefits worth becoming excited over. We are reminded of the elderly New England clergyman that Herbert W. Hansen told about, who touched upon the various degrees of thanksgiving in his family prayer:

O Lord, as you know very well, here we are again. We are here to do one of the hardest things any mortal can do—to give thanks and really mean it. First of all, there are those people who don't ever say thanks for anything because they figure that whatever they have, they got it all by themselves. Then there are those who do give thanks for things received, but you can catch something in their voices that asks, "And why didn't I get it sooner?" And there are those who also say thanks but imply, "Why didn't I get more?"

How sorry, then, is the whole business of living if gratitude has no place in it! It is a dry and shallow affair from which the joys of creativity and achievement have fled. On the other hand, Halyburton, the Scottish saint, once described thanksgiving as an antidote to barrenness of soul, "When I am in the lowest depths I can pull myself back into the sunshine through the duty of thankfulness." In so speaking he was merely reflecting what Scripture has always taught and witnessed to concerning the grateful life.

How full the Bible is of praise and thanksgiving! Our greatest heritage from Hebrew worship was their hymnbook, their Book of Psalms, and if anyone wished seriously to know the meaning of gratitude he or she could always find it there. "Praise the Lord!" said the psalmist, "For it is good to sing praises to our God; he is gracious, and a song of praise is seemly" (Ps. 147:1). Moreover, early Christian worship was named the Eucharist, the Greek word for "thanksgiving," and this service was marked by joy and praise in honor of the resurrection. How impressively these two emphases, Hebrew and Christian, are brought together into a great crescendo in the traditional Scottish service of Holy Communion when the congregation in closing sings the paraphrase of Psalm 103:

> O Thou, my soul, bless God the Lord;
> And all that in me is
> Be stirred up his holy name
> To magnify and bless!

From what we have said thus far some right notions about

thanksgiving begin to emerge. The late Carl Sandburg was asked one day what he thought of modern poetry, and he replied, "Too much of it is cerebral; it is poetry of the mind, not of the blood." Real thanksgiving cannot be discussed or understood as a mental theory, nor can it ever be a solitary experience reserved for and turned on only on Sunday; it must be a prevailing attitude toward life. And as such it inevitably raises such ultimate questions as "To whom?" and "What for?" Genuine thanksgiving can never be an academic matter or a command performance on the great occasion; its habitat is the life's blood of men and women who have found in God the only satisfying answer to the basic questions and mysteries of their existence. William Law asked, "Who is the greatest saint in the world?" In answering his own question he wrote:

> It is not he who prays most or fasts most; it is not he who gives most alms, or is most eminent for temperance, chastity, or justice; *but* it is he who is always thankful to God, who receives everything as an instance of God's goodness and has a heart always ready to praise God for it. [1]

This is real thanksgiving, and in no place have its complexion and essence been spelled out with such originality and care as in Psalm 103, where the ancient writer calls upon his own soul, "Bless the Lord . . . and all that is within me, bless his holy name." But what made his kind of thanksgiving reflect the direction and mood of his own life was his knowledge of God. His firsthand experience of who and what God is kindled this spontaneous song of praise and gratitude.

The first lesson we learn from Psalm 103 is that *real thanksgiving involves our whole being.* "All that is within me, bless his holy name" is the demand of the psalmist. In his thinking, thanksgiving would be a truncated affair if it consisted merely of the singing of a hymn, or a national holiday once a year, or a thoughtless sense of satisfaction in believing that somehow God has blessed only the Anglo-Saxon race. Thanksgiving is more than a wave of superficial emotionalism. It embraces and emerges from the exercise of the mind and will also. This is why the old commandment names first of all God's record of good will to God's creation and then denotes "You shall love the Lord your God with . . . heart, . . . soul, . . . and mind." Indeed, the Bible implies that this kind of thanksgiving alone should be the ideal of each of us, because of its power to provide our whole motive for living.

So much of our dealings with God, life, and destiny implicate only a fraction of our being. Take prayer, for example. So much of it is occupied only with petition, which is generally a rehearsal or catalogue of our own selfish ends; so little of it is praise and thanksgiving. Petition is the lowest form of prayer, because its focus is constantly upon our own needs and concerns. Thanksgiving, on the other hand, is the highest form, because it tends to lift us up into freedom from self, and through glorying in God and God's goodness we see our dependence upon God and what we can become when we take God seriously.

The psalmist, however, indicates that the wholeness of this kind of thanksgiving springs, not from what God has done *for* humankind, but chiefly for what God has done *in* humankind. The psalmist does not add up potatoes, pumpkins, and apples to see if this year's crop merits more thanksgiving than last. On the contrary, he names what God has done in us as the things for which he is thankful primarily: God forgives, heals, redeems, crowns, satisfies, and renews. God is a God of mercy who gets at our sinful nature, at our rebellious hearts, and at all that is ugly and unholy, removing it as far as the east is from the west. The psalmist knew that peace of mind and rebirth of soul—the essence of the new life—were gifts to be cherished more than all the fruits of the field. Only those who turn to God, only they who thus know life in all its rich dimensions, are able to offer meaningful thanksgiving. "All that is within me" is really all a person is in his or her character, personal power, and spiritual potential. Thanksgiving means our joyful offering back to God of all God has made of us. This is the supreme motive of the Christian life and it is renewed and clarified every time we bless the Lord so truly that we lose ourselves in wonder, love, and praise.

The second lesson this psalm impresses upon us is that *real thanksgiving begins with what God is rather than what humankind is.*

The psalmist never began by thanking God for what he himself was. He praised God first of all for what God is and for what God has done for God's people.

> He made known his ways to Moses, his acts to the people of Israel. The Lord is merciful and gracious, slow to anger, and abounding in steadfast love. . . . He does not deal with us according to our sins, nor requite us according to our iniquities. For as the heavens are high above the earth, so great is his steadfast love toward those who fear him. . . . As a father pities his children, so the Lord pities those who fear him. . . . The steadfast love of the Lord is from everlasting to everlasting upon those who fear him. (vv. 7–13, 17)

How very differing it was with the pagan religions! They feared their gods. In terror they offered endless sacrifices in order to appease an angry and slighted god. And they went away from their religious exercises in the same frantic state in which they came. But the psalmist lifted up his adoring heart to a God who was utter holiness, goodness, mercy, and truth, and went out from that presence into his service as both a humbler and a bigger man: humbler, because he knew what he himself was as compared with God; bigger, because an abiding sense of God's great goodness would now interpenetrate his own little life. "The basis of all great living," said Farmer, "is reverence." Real thanksgiving embodies reverence. We are most likely to be sincere in our thanksgiving if its spirit is infused with a sense of reverent wonder before the One whose love was so amazing that it demands everything we are in return.

A further lesson the psalmist shares with us is that *real thanksgiving depends upon the extent to which we do God's will.*

We should note the characteristic phrases the psalmist uses: "to those who keep his covenant"; "who do his word"; "hearkening to the voice of his word." The implication here is that thanksgiving is never a duty to be legislated; it is the joyous satisfaction that comes from doing what is right and good through the enabling will of God who wants to make us what we ought to be. Thanksgiving is allied, then, with surrender and freedom: surrender to God and freedom from self. Without these, thanksgiving is an empty thing, as it is for the average American: a day on which to eat one's fill and wallow in affluence the underprivileged of our world have never imagined. Some years ago a cartoon in *The New Yorker* pictured a well-dressed, wealthy lady seated on a divan at an exclusive seaside hotel turning to her husband and saying, "Wouldn't this be perfect, if it weren't for Russia?" Might she not say today, "Wouldn't this be a perfect Thanksgiving were it not for . . . El Salvador . . . the Arabs . . . the blacks?" Like the Pharisee in the temple, we tend to thank God for what we have individually, but the "fly in the ointment" is this Publican whose presence upsets things by forcing our thinking about thanksgiving out of the realm of smug indulgence and confronting us with the challenge of doing God's will in community.

Edwin Arlington Robinson, in his *Captain Craig*, Part I, wrote, "Two kinds of gratitude: the sudden kind we feel for what we take, the larger kind we feel for what we give." Taking is more likely under the pressure of one's own will. Giving is usually in response to a need and will outside our own. Jesus condemned those who cried "Lord, Lord" but who did not follow through with the doing of God's will. Moreover, in the New Testament, whenever Jesus is said to have offered thanks to God, it was with relation to the giving of himself in the doing of the Father's will and to the spiritual satisfaction this relationship supplied.

Amy Carmichael, who gave her whole life with radiant joy and satisfaction for the untouchables in India, said that her decision to venture upon such a precarious mission came from hearing a lay person pray simply, "We thank Thee, Lord, that Thou art able." This is the message of the psalmist: that heart is most truly thankful who, having accepted what he or she feels to be God's will for him or her, finds that all the resources of heaven are backing him or her up. Paul would describe this state of mind and heart as "joy and peace in believing." If we bring God honestly into our thanksgiving, we shall still bless God's name for what God is and does, but with a difference—we shall appropriate God's will as we do God's commandments and become ourselves a blessing to others in our time.

Pericope: Exodus 3:1-20

Worksheet 1

This pericope is a vignette: the seen encountered by the Unseen. The medium: an ordinary bush on fire. The ordinary seized by the extraordinary. Note Moses' respect in the face of the inexplicable. The holy meant something to them in those days: something the human shrank from. The encounter was individual but its effect was social. A purpose revealed here. Accompanied by a promise. An obligation must be fulfilled. The old spiritual has it: "Go down, Moses" into Egypt's land. God is always supportive if the purpose is God's will. Old Testament calls had certain common features, similar pattern. Note Moses had an eye for this peculiar phenomenon. "I will turn aside . . ." Not indifferent. God's revelations often come through commonplace. Not a bolt of lightning from the heavens. Elizabeth Browning's lines: "Earth's crammed with heaven, / And every common bush afire with God; / And only he who sees takes off his shoes— / The rest sit round it and pluck blackberries" ("Aurora Leigh," book 7, line 820). Note how God identifies God self as the God of the whole human family (v. 15). God works through an individual; through the one to the many. Anyone who feels life's demand is too big for him- or herself is more apt to measure up to it than those who deal with life flippantly. Each one has his or her special work to do. Delineate what is God's business and what is our own. The former is more likely to be fraught with high purpose and when one submits to it, it becomes the stuff of a destiny.

Worksheet 2

Moses flees into the land of Midian when he fears the aftermath of his slaying the Egyptian. He marries into the family of Jethro, a priest of Midian, and tends his flocks. One day he is encountered by God in the well-known incident of the burning bush and is commissioned with a message from God both to the Egyptian Pharaoh and his own people, the enslaved Israelites.

The nature of Moses' call tells us more about God than about him. God takes the initiative because God is concerned with and about God's own people. The chosen person in this case is to become the agent for God's purpose and he is an ordinary man in very ordinary circumstances. The burning bush is not in itself a determinative symbol. God speaks a word to Moses who, after some initial demurring, becomes ready to listen and to act. His shrinking from the assignment dissolves with God's assurance of a supply of power. The whole venture is underwritten by the integrity of God's name. Moses becomes a "sent" person and his mission is defined. Israel in due course would become an instrument of redemption in God's purpose and hands.

Commentaries: *The Book of Exodus*, by S. R. Driver (Cambridge: Cambridge University Press, 1953); *The Book of Exodus*, by A. H. McNeile (London: Methuen & Co., 1931); *Exodus*, by B. S. Childs (Philadelphia: Westminster Press, 1974); and *The Book of Exodus*, by J. P. Hyatt (London: Oliphantes, 1971).

Central Idea: Ours is a secular environment. Our danger lies in allowing ourselves to belong only to it and thereby what we are will never be more than its dimensions prescribe. Our horizon is constricted then to what we are to the exclusion of what we can be. In God's eyes and purpose we are more than where and what we are now; life has another dimension which is above and beyond the secular and can transform it by giving to our living a new direction, meaning, and purpose.

Point of Immediacy: The message concerns and is directed to persons whose lives are being lived in terms of material aims and ends and whose dissatisfaction with these things as they are is painfully real.

Text: Exodus 3:1–20

Topic: "God Captures the Secular Person"

Sermonic Sample

Near the end of the nineteenth century a little book appeared, written by Edwin Abbott, entitled *Flatland.* It was the story of a world of two dimensions: a world of length and breadth, but no height. How many persons there are today who live in this kind of world! A two-dimensional world—a world of surfaces from which no one ever looks up. They are very much like a great European house of entertainment about which someone said, "The lights of the music hall have blotted out the stars." A good description of our age? Georgia Harkness remarked: "Secularism is the organization of life as if God did not exist." Consider the barrenness of modern life. Aims and ends have length and breadth but little height. Wordsworth's sonnet aptly described this kind of living:

> The world is too much with us
> Late and soon, getting and spending
> We lay waste our powers.

But we cannot rid ourselves of the secular. Monasticism is not the solution. We have to live in it. It is part of the fabric of our existence. God did not intend our submission to the secular, God knows we must live within it, but God's intention is that our direction, calling, and ends must come from beyond it. Remember H. G. Wells's character in *The Research Magnificent*, a young man who regarded life as one long succession of days, of simply filling in with the secular routine, sensing a pattern of flatness on every hand, until finally he cried out, "O God, give me back my visions!"

We turn now to the Moses incident. Here is an ordinary man in an ordinary job. Not a superman. Yet a man sensitive to human need and suffering; ready to listen; open-minded; lonely and searching for some handle by which to grasp life. Suddenly God strikes ("a flame of fire") . . . a burning bush . . . an inquiring mind ("I will turn aside") . . . God speaks ("Moses, Moses") . . . a call to a reverent and devotional posture ("Put off your shoes . . . holy ground") . . . Moses is overwhelmed . . . but God's nature, not his own, makes the difference between a dead-end life and an expanding horizon, between meaninglessness and purposefulness.

When God captures the secular person, God tells us something about God self. The theoretical God, the God of abstract discussion, the God of the philosophical equation is dead—and deserves to be so. But the Bible presents again and again incidents where God takes the initiative because God is concerned: "I have seen their affliction and have come down." Here is a God who deals with human souls. "I am the God of Abraham . . ."— God's influence and action have been known in specific instances; God had written God's own record. A composite picture took shape from God's actions in history. No other god could do this. Billy Graham once quipped about the "God is dead" movement of the 1960s: "God is not dead; I talked with him this morning." God's nature is learned only in the depths of authentic Christian experience. God's province is the secular, but wherever and whenever God comes into the human scene and receives a sincere response, that place becomes for us holy ground; that is, who and what God is creates before us a time-space event that shakes the flatness of ordinary living and lifts it to the level of higher purpose.

When God captures the secular person, God tells us something of what God thinks of us. God craves the open mind. This was the case of Moses: God and man became the man of God. Once the assignment is put—"I will send you"—no one any longer belongs to him- or herself. What is more, no one any longer operates on his or her own: "I will be with you." You and I are sent out with power to do. The summons comes; we must act. Moses, the secular person, is captured by God; he gets a new grip upon himself as he catches new vistas of his real vocation and of his potential to exercise it. Motivation, direction, duty, and the like, become second nature to one who initially shrank back from the prospect. "Who am I?" is counteracted by "I have sent you." As someone said, "God sends no persons on errands which he does not give them power to do." Not Pharaoh versus Moses, but Pharaoh versus Moses *plus* Another. Not is Moses able? God with Moses and we have another situation entirely.

When God captures the secular person, God tells us something of God's intention for our destiny. When God called Moses, the shepherd, from caring for Jethro's flocks, God's intention was that Moses should inform the people of God's plan for their destiny. Indeed, this call was to indicate that this world was subject to God and was not merely the arena for injustice, slavery, and cruelty. Again Moses is hesitant, not on account of his own gifts this time, but about "selling the idea" to his own people. Who is this God? What is God's name? Does God really have an edge over all the other gods? Moses did not want to go to his people saying "God sent me," unless he could lay the integrity of this God on the line. "What is his name?" "I am who I am" or more exactly "I will be what I will be." What is this—a play on words? No, it was in keeping with the Old Testament idea that a "name" and a "character" had a common identification.

God's assurance, therefore, to Moses and his people was that God's promises were endorsed by and with God's own integrity; and most important—God will be for them to whatever extent the measure of their commitment to God will permit. They were given a blank check, endorsed with God's name, and the amount could be filled in according to the proportion of their faithfulness. God is such that our future is ours, but its greatness will lie in the extent to which we make it God's. George Matheson, in his hymn "Make Me a Captive, Lord," sang:

> My will is not my own
> Till thou hast made it thine;
> If it would reach a monarch's throne
> It must its crown resign;
> It only stands unbent
> Amid the clashing strife,
> When on thy bosom it has leant
> And found in thee its life.[5]

Pericope: The Book of Jonah

Worksheet 1

Authorship difficult to establish. Really a drama. Whoever wrote it shared much of the Old Testament prophetic substance and tradition. Echoes and intimations here of universalism; suggestive of Deutero-Isaiah. Struggle here between national narrowness and broader world concern. A hangover here from the exile: only human that they hoped God, by some vengeful act, would wipe out those who caused such suffering to God's own people. Maybe Jonah thought similarly. Strong missionary motif here. Concept of chosenness cast into a new light: elected not to privilege but to service. Jonah shrank from assignment; most prophets did. Escapism is only human. Maybe he welcomed the storm (1:4–6). Popular story in which focus is too much and mistakenly on a whale. Much is left to imagination. The drama has, according to Aristotle, "a beginning, a middle, and an end." The ending, from Jonah's viewpoint, may appear to us as flat. An element of superstition here and there; for example, the crew's decision to throw Jonah overboard. Note a characteristic about God: demanding obedience but yet ready to forgive. Jonah's second call has hints of the idea of a second chance. Drama has its own surprises: Jonah is an instant success, whereas missionary campaigns are usually slow. A shock to Israelite prejudice. God's grace has a universal claim. We miss God's Word to us because our discernment is clouded by our human faults and misgivings. A call in life can be the experience of any good person. There is an against-ness in the makeup of every prophet. Ordinary occasions have sometimes great reverberations. If one is right with God, he or she is not likely to do anything wrong. There is no escape from God. Francis Thompson's poem "The Hound of Heaven."

Worksheet 2

A commentator has said, "Jonah is a book about God and his servant Jonah; not a book by Jonah." Book is an account of the mission of Jonah. (Ref. in 2 Kings 14:25.) Jonah was a direct successor to Elijah and Elisha and a senior contemporary of Amos and Hosea. Book was not written in eighth century, because Nineveh did not fall until 606 B.C. Internal evidence dates the book about 300 B.C. Author was apparently someone who protested the provincialism of the Jewish church compared with the breadth of God's love.

Missionary emphasis is strong here. Someone drew up an acrostic from the contents of the book: running from God (chap. 1), running to God (chap. 2), running with God (chap. 3), and running ahead of God (chap. 4). Clever, but a measure of truth here. One lesson: God's grace reaches the heathen despite the refusal of God's people to recognize their mission to them (cf. Acts 11). Curious: the message of Jonah is for Nineveh, but its lesson is for Israel. God called Jonah, but he tried to run out on God; he is roundly condemned for his action. God calls a second time. Jonah acts, somewhat reluctantly. He does not really like the outcome. The drama points up God's love and concern for all peoples.

Commentaries: *Ruth and Jonah*, by G. A. F. Knight (London: SCM Press, 1950); *Jonah*, by Jacques Ellul (Grand Rapids: Wm. B. Eerdmans, 1971); *Jonah*, by T. T. Perowne (Cambridge:

Cambridge University Press, 1879); *Jonah*, M. M. Kalisch (London: Longmans, Green & Co., 1878); *Jonah*, by A. D. Martin (London: Longmans, Green & Co., 1926); *The Minor Prophets*, by A. Maclaren (Grand Rapids; Wm. B. Eerdmans, 1952); *The Book of the Twelve Prophets*, vol. II, by G. A. Smith (New York: A. C. Armstrong & Son, 1901).

Central Idea: Over against our prejudice, exclusiveness, and intolerance, God lays a claim—sometimes dramatically—upon the usefulness to God of our love, especially when it is measured and inspired by God's.

Point of Immediacy: Message is directed to a human situation: the presence in any congregation of conscious and unconscious attitudes of prejudice toward others.

Text: Jonah 1, 3, and 4.

Topic: "God's Campaign against Human Prejudice"

Strategy: Elicit from the Jonah drama a moral and spiritual principle as a guideline for action and as an example in the face of misjudgments of others.

Sermonic Sample

The Bible speaks out strongly against human prejudice. It appears in the exclusive person, the closed mind, the bigot, and in such examples as the Pharisees, high priests, the elder brother. These types are among the hardest to deal with, chiefly because their righteousness is a legalistic form of morality and their stubborn will holds out against the realization of God's wider plan.

It was to this kind of person that the call of God came when in the scheme of things a voice arrested the prophet Jonah. (Insert here the substance of the drama: Jonah is called to preach to Nineveh. Not willingly. Fled to Joppa to embark for Tarshish.

Storm. Heathen sailors acquit themselves more admirably than he. Capitulates to their will. Dumped overboard. The fish. Got shore leave. Called by God again. Acted. It worked. Jonah is upset. God's purpose and power are seen not only in the conversion of heathen Nineveh, but in the contrast with the figure Jonah had cut: "That is why I made haste to flee to Tarshish; for I knew that thou art a gracious God and merciful, slow to anger, and abounding in steadfast love, and repentest of evil" [4:2].)

God's call and Jonah's response teach us several lessons that have contemporary relevance:

We cannot run out on God. Francis Thompson's poem "The Hound of Heaven" has been used to illustrate humanity's flight from God, and God's unerring pursuit:

> I fled him, down the nights and down the days;
> I fled him, down the arches of the years;
> I fled him, down the labyrinthine ways
> Of my own mind . . .[6]

No more nor less graphic was Jonah's flight. And us? Maybe not so dramatic, but equally real, shameful, and demoralizing. We shrink from the demand of God's encounter, but our escape hatch is not always on the deck of a ship. Either (1) we try to reduce God to our own size by erasing his "otherness" in order to make him manageable (like Jacob at Bethel, we say, "If you will . . . then I"). Or (2) we attempt to imagine for ourselves a "godless" world, to be rid of the goads of conscience, moral sanctions, community judgments, and the like. But, like Jonah, we discover that the rabble (the sailors on the Joppa ship) fear a deity, exhibit decency, worship (though clumsily), and work with good intentions. Thus we, like Jonah, appear as the godless ones. Or (3) we busy ourselves with life's options so that we avoid a face-to-face encounter and the demand it entails. Many people bypass the church today because they are more scared to come than indifferent to it. There is nothing disturbing to be expected in the secular—except war and poverty—and after all, these are the business of Congress. But then it happens! God is seen in a need. This explains a Moses, an Elijah, an Ezekiel—biblical figures; or a Schweitzer, a John Geddie, a Tom Dooley, a Mother Teresa—all of whom could not avoid God's claim.

Our call from God is not to privilege, but to service. Jonah was of the elect: privileged, exclusive, narrow, and willful. Prejudice and privilege make friends easily. Their cry is "rights" and "preferences" rather than duties. Characteristics: at ease because everything, including their God, is localized and traditional. And us? Does our God have any concern for politics, social wrongs, or human deprivation, or the Ninevehs not "of our kind"? Why should persons of privilege risk their reputation and security in a plan for "outsiders" that might not be a good idea at all? This need not be the eighth century; it could be the twentieth. Jonah felt elect, but these rough sailors had more sympathy than he. The people of Nineveh were miserable heathens, but their response to God was immediate. Jonah wore the badge of "servant of God," yet he hated those whom God loved and he wanted only to be a witness to their destruction. He was to learn—as we must too—that God's Word is not necessarily a privilege for one person and doom for another, but a call to serve and extend God's purpose.

We are not blessed for our own sake, but for others' sakes. How disturbing to Jonah must have been God's persistent calls! He had national pride: these Assyrians were a constant threat to Israel and should not be given a chance anyway. He had personal pride: his own reputation would be laid upon the line. What if this missionary excursion to Nineveh were to flop? Either way seemed to make no sense—except maybe one should get out of the bind because, after all, concern for one's own lot comes first. "What we have we hold" was the old maxim. But should we? Jew and Assyrian were equal in the sight of God. But the Jew had a religious treasure the Assyrians thus far did not own. What is the mind, purpose, and will of God in all this? Was Israel's heritage something to hoard selfishly with an aura of smugness or was God telling them to break down the walls of prejudice and share their spiritual bounty with others? "For my own sake"—take the Tarshish boat and escape? Or for others' sakes—repent in the dungeon of despair and come out and accept God's call anew? Our answer is determined by how much we know the love of God.

5
The Servant Preaching

Frequently during homiletics workshops and in the seminary classrooms, students or pastors ask: Is it right to do this or wrong to do that in constructing a sermon? This, however, is the wrong question. It implies an attempt to live and operate strictly by a set of rules and this can be a sure way to inhibit your own art, individuality, originality, and spontaneity. Far better is it to heed a few principles that guarantee effectiveness, impact, decision, and a dynamic meeting of mind with mind.

Suppose Winston Churchill, for example, had written his wartime speeches (1941–45) strictly according to the rules of the book with an eye particularly to the minutiae of grammar and syntax. Think of the situation: the imminent invasion of the British Isles by the Nazi armies and Churchill's need to lift the whole nation to a new level of courage and the will to endure. His secret weapon was the use of words. The rules of the book would have produced a speech exhorting the people, Let us be brave! But it was the artist in Churchill who said, "We shall fight on the landing grounds; we shall fight in the fields and in the streets; we shall fight in the hills; we shall never surrender! And suppose this Empire were to live 1,000 years, men shall still say, 'This was their finest hour!' " The art of speaking in this way galvanized the will of the nation to resist and to maintain themselves as the last stronghold of European liberty.

In the opinion of this writer, there are six qualities or characteristics every sermon should have in order to assure maximum effectiveness. Two sermons, one following the book and the other attempting to engage the interest of the congregation, one homiletically foolproof and the other person-directed, may register entirely different results. The former may elicit the reactions Richard Borden talks about: "Ho hum! Why bring that up? For instance? [i.e., prove it with an example.] So what!"[1] In other words, there are certain reasons why one sermon is good and another bad; why one "rings the bell" and another wrecks the budget; why one works a miracle, whereas of the other, the verdict is "the operation was successful, but the patient died."

Let us discuss six sermonic characteristics without which your sermon and mine on any Sunday morning are apt to fail to communicate the Word to people who need it. To assist in the implementation of these, we must put them in the form of principles.

BE PERSONAL

Be direct. A young lad hearing Spurgeon preach turned to his mother and remarked, "That man is talking to me." Part of the secret of this kind of thing is eye contact. If there is one thing television has taught preachers it is that eye contact is essential. Absence of eye contact on the part of a television speaker spells disaster. Television programming is arranged for the intimacy of across-the-room distances where eye contact is imperative. But frequently, even with a teleprompter, communication is botched by someone whose line of vision is too high or too low.

This point has to do, of necessity, with smaller situations and contexts. But what about the large assembly or the spacious church sanctuary where the features of the speaker are not always distinct? the nave of a great cathedral? a college chapel? a political convention? Directness has to be achieved here by other means.

Directness must be infused into the preacher's writing style. Alexander Maclaren, who filled Manchester's Baptist Church twice on Sundays for almost four decades, placed an empty chair at the opposite side of his study desk and as he prepared his sermon he talked aloud every sentence with an imaginery parishioner before him. This gave his sermons a dialogical character at their very inception. For this reason, Fosdick cautioned young preachers, "Write for hearers, not for readers."

Directness must be gained from a built-in "I-thou" relationship. There is you and the congregation. You must set up with them a sense of personal rapport. Norman Vincent Peale and Robert H. Schuller do it admirably. It is achieved partly through choice of pronouns. Use "you" and "I" rather than "we." Avoid the abstract: "man," "one," "they," and "people." Avoid wherever possible the impersonal "one" ("one sees," "one has said," or "someone wrote somewhere"). Do not be afraid to use "I" occasionally. Television preachers do not shrink from using "I." Paul Scherer once remarked, "If you have to use the pronoun 'I,' for pity sakes use it, and don't walk around on the stilts of some substitute."

Directness must be the result of an awareness of who your hearers are. Charles Kingsley would lean over the pulpit on Sunday morning and say, "Here we are again to talk about what is really going on in your soul and mine." In this way he recognized the fact that the congregation was there and he had common ties with them in the struggles of life. This is what the media of our time call "audience orientation." It is one of the basic and necessary keys to effective preaching.

Use proper names. This does not mean name-dropping or saying, "The other day I had luncheon with the Sheik of Iraq who owns 150 oil wells in the Persian Gulf and who said to me, 'I owe all my success in life to your one book, *The Art of Seizing upon Possibilities.*' " But it does mean: beware of being academic. In sermonizing one must never discuss abstract principles per se; incorporate them in persons. The Bible never traffics in abstractions. Take, for example, Hebrews 11, where the writer is not content merely to say, "Faith is the assurance of things hoped for, the conviction of things not seen." He goes on: "By faith Abraham . . . by faith Jacob . . . by faith Moses. . . ." Step by step he proceeds with one concrete fact after another from history, until we reach the climactic verses of chapter 12, "Therefore, since we are surrounded by so great a cloud of witnesses, let us also lay aside every weight, and sin which clings so closely, and let us run with perseverance the race that is set before us, looking to Jesus . . ."

Newspaper reports are adept at this kind of thing: they seek out proper names to make the story personal. So also in preaching, none of us should speak of a human quality or doctrine without showing it *alive* in a person. The old illustration is pertinent here which tells of the mother who assured her little daughter not to fear when the light was switched off in her bedroom, for God would oversee and take care of her. But the tiny voice remonstrated, "But I want a God with a face!" When Jesus wanted to teach brotherly and sisterly love, it was not enough to say, "Thou shalt love . . ." He brought in a person; "A man was going down from Jerusalem to Jericho . . ." (Luke 10:25–37). People then saw the principle come alive. A somewhat redundant remark by a teacher of preaching had a measure of truth in it, "People your sermons with people." It has to be names that mean something to the hearers, however. There was a time when religious heroes were Schweitzer, Dooley, Dag Hammerskjold, Kagawa of Japan, J. R. Mott, and others, but not today. Barth's dictum applies here: "The preacher must prepare with the Bible in one hand and the newspaper in the other."

Create interest. One of the great weaknesses of much modern preaching is that it is not interesting. Spurgeon said about one preacher, "He would make a good martyr; he was so dry he'd burn well." Or it was said about one Anglican bishop, "He was so heavenly minded, he was of no earthly use." Whatever one may say about the preaching of Peale and Schuller, they never fail to be interesting. Their aim at the very outset of every sermon is to stimulate interest. Before the preacher every Sunday morning are several hundred wandering minds with diverse and fleeting foci. Hence, the preacher must say something that will grab them right off. Remember their attention response and span are influenced and determined by watching and hearing six weekdays of television commercials. Peale was speaking on "Lose Your Fears through Faith" and he began: "Would you like to lose your fears? Of course, you would. And you can. The way to do it is through faith." Or George Buttrick announced his text, John 14:7: "It is expedient for you that I go away." Then, turning to his perceptive Madison Avenue congregation in New York City, he began: "Do you believe that? No, of course you don't. . . ." None of us must assume that people come to church simply bursting to hear us speak. More often than not they sit back in the pews, fold their spiritual arms, and say within themselves, "Well, what have you got to say this morning that will interest me?"

Incidentally, you and I must remember that there is a common need in all women and men to whom you and I preach. Never ought we to think that those before us are all crackpots, schizophrenics, sadists, masochists, or what have you. The majority are healthy folk in body and mind. Edwin Dahlberg, an outstanding Baptist preacher of a generation ago and one-time president of the National Council of Churches, was talking to a group of Midwestern preachers and he remarked, "Don't give the impression to your people that it is their duty to have a problem, to be all mixed up and confused, in order to be in style psychologically. Many of them are extremely happy and are not interested in doom and gloom."

Joseph Pulitzer, the founder and originator of the prize for journalism that bears his name, said to a group of American news writers, "Put it before them briefly so they will read it; clearly so they will appreciate it; picturesquely so they will remember it; and above all, accurately so they may be guided by its light."

BE PICTORIAL

Incidentally, there is no one way to do a sermon that is sacrosanct. The reason one sermon may be effective may be quite different from the reason another is or is not. No teacher of preachers should attempt to pour everyone into the same mold.

Nor should any preacher her- or himself set another up as a model to be aped or duplicated to the last gesture. Trevor H. Davies, the great Welsh-Canadian preacher, remarked to a group of seminary students, "I was never so consciously a complete failure as when I tried to imitate someone else."

We might look at it this way: every complete sentence consists of a subject, verb, and object. But what makes your sentence yours and my sentence mine depends upon the following: the content we put into it; the originality of words we use; the sequence in which we place these words for emphasis and effect; the color of the word choice (abstract, concrete, warm, or human); and the mood (elementary, questioning, etc.). It is the same with a sermon; the basic principles may be the same, but what makes my sermon mine and yours yours are the differences we named regarding sentences. Aristotle said that every drama must have "a beginning, a middle, and an end." And so has every drama had ever since. But this is not to say that all dramas are the same and that all dramatists operate in the same way. Take, for example, this memorable sentence, this classic by Winston Churchill about the Royal Air Force's acquittal in the desperate Battle of Britain in 1941, "Never in the field of human conflict was so much owed by so many to so few." This declaration has found its echo in countless orations, religious and political, ever since. But suppose Churchill had put it this way: "So many have never owed so much to so few in the field of human conflict." Would such a sentence find its way memorably into the fabric of rhetorical literature?

When we talk, however, about pictorial language or vocabulary we do not mean flowery words, high-flown lines, or what the Victorians used to call "purple patches." It means we ought to have variety, color, imagination, figures of speech, and literary allusions from mutually understood contexts. Robert J. McCracken always maintained that every preacher must be a student of words. To be imaginative is a necessity and one's tools are words. Most of the great pulpit personalities excelled here

(Brooks, Henry Ward Beecher, Parker, Leslie D. Weatherhead, Arthur J. Gossip, Scherer, and others). Some used imaginative power in an anecdote or illustration. Others used living figures of speech by means of simile, metaphor, or an exciting image in a single phrase. Some words have color in themselves and require no modifiers, for example, words like "destiny," "landslide," "dynamic," "wreck," "refuge," "shambles," "fireproof," "spineless." Words like these turn your congregation's ears into eyes. Moreover, when adjectives or adverbs are used they should be vivid and real, never from the vague stratosphere, but from the average run of common life that is readily understood. The preacher must zero in upon the people's level of understanding, avoiding what is either too high or too low. James Denney once remarked, "The man who shoots above the target does not prove thereby he has superior ammunition. He just proves he can't shoot." At the other extreme is the preacher who said, "I just spread the fodder out on the ground where anything from a giraffe to a jackass can get it." If certain words are emotion-packed, certainly they require no qualification, for example, "hate," "violence," "urgency," "betrayal," "drive," "thrust," "siege," or "monstrous."

Two examples indicate the strength of impact the choice and sequence of words can make in the reporting of a similar incident. Here is the prodigal (Luke 15:18, 19): "I will arise and go to my father, and I will say to him, 'Father, I have sinned against heaven and before you; I am no longer worthy to be called your son; treat me as one of your hired servants.'" Note this paraphrase: "I am determined to go to my dear aged parent, and try to excite his tenderness and compassion for me. I will kneel before him and accost him in these penitent and pathetic terms: 'O, best of parents! I acknowledge myself an ungrateful creature to heaven and to you. Condescend to hire me in the capacity of the meanest slave.' " Does anyone believe that if Jesus had said it this way it would ever have been remembered? Incidentally, two of our more skillful writers of this kind of thing in the contemporary pulpit are Frederick B. Speakman and Ernest T. Campbell. Here are a few examples from Speakman's *The Salty Tang:* "The lay people who determine the rate of the church's heartbeat." "We've made a cult of pace." "There's a dry rasping sob at the heart of all our modern doubts, in spite of our blasé bluff." "They threw some rags of mock purple over his pulped and bleeding shoulders."[2] Or, Campbell: "To suggest that man is inert, like a piece of chewing gum, rolling around in the jaws of history."

BE PROPULSIVE

A sermon ought to bear a certain resemblance to a power line or telephone line going up a hillside. The first pole represents the initial idea and the line to the next pole is its development, and so on, pole by pole, the stream of thought is furthered (each pole represents the rounding out of an idea and the continuous line the thrust of the theme) until the peak or climax is reached and the final pole is anchored at the summit. The purpose of any sermon is to move the people from where they are to where they ought to be. This is done by the sheer momentum of the sermon's logic; by its pursuit of a goal or solution; by its ability to carry the people along to a decision; and by its pointing them to a place beyond their reach. In what sense? (1) In the sense of mission: the great Welsh preacher, Richard Roberts, for example, speaking before a large assembly of students in the University of Toronto, lifted them all up to a new vision of the Christian mission and at the climax of his address he said, "Go now, each of you, and transact this great business for yourself." (2) In the sense of an expanding vision: Turner, the painter, seated on the seashore, was attempting to paint a picture of the ocean, and finally he threw down his brush in despair and said, "It keeps growing greater and greater; I cannot ever paint it." There is a sense in which the more we know the gospel and the more we see it at work among humankind, the more the vision expands. The love and grace of God are too vast for our little minds to grasp fully and, therefore, all our sermons can do is to point to their ever-growing dimensions.

BE PASTORAL

Preachers ride some words or terms to death. Between 1940 and 1945 the word was "challenge." From 1945 to 1950, "rapport." From 1950 to 1960, "relevance." During the 1960s there was a whole host of them, such as "does he or she relate?" (No one pointed out that "relate" is not an intransitive verb!) Then "involvement" became the "in" word. For a time the word "cope" was on everybody's lips (late seventies and early eighties). President McCord of Princeton Theological Seminary torpedoed the latter when he said, "We who are ordained to proclaim the abundant life are reduced to telling people to cope. Coping means being able to get through the day and then, having made it, we pull the blankets up over us and say, 'Well, we've survived!' " There will be many other "in" words, but those that will be most viable and apt are ones that imply and connote pastoral insight and concern. Halford Luccock called this "the tact that makes for contact." Eighty years ago, Norman MacLeod was minister in a village church in Scotland and an elder of the session was a blacksmith. Every morning as MacLeod fetched his mail in town he passed the blacksmith's shop and he dropped by for a chat. "He never came into my shop," said the blacksmith, "without talking as if he himself had been a blacksmith all his life."

The key to such pastoral involvement is *empathy*. What is empathy? Few have defined it more clearly than Farmer, "It is the power to penetrate objectively yet feelingly (not emotionally) into the individual self-awareness of any man with whom we have to deal—so that in some measure we get inside his skin, see the world through his eyes, hear the world through his ears, participate in his feelings, think his thoughts, get a sense of him as an individual with only one life to live, one death to die."[3] It was said of John Henry Newman's preaching, "He laid his finger—how gently, yet how powerfully!—on some inner place in the hearer's heart, and told him things about himself he had never known until then."[1]

It has become increasingly difficult today to preach effectively and at the same time not to be a pastor. The old aphorism
was "A house-going pastor makes a church-going people." However, an effective pastoral visit is not what was said about one
minister who was called "ring and run"—before the resident
reached the door in answer to the bell, the pastor was already
down the street. When Buttrick was minister of the Madison
Avenue Presbyterian Church there were four members on the
clergy staff. Each minister was responsible for two organizations
and eight hundred pastoral calls a year. A seasoned clergyman,
addressing a class of graduating seminarians, said, "If you are
not interested in people, you will have a tough time in the ministry."

BE PERSUASIVE

Basic to all preaching is to persuade the congregation to adopt
the Christian way of life. It is a matter of changing their attitudes and consequently their actions by supplanting their old
beliefs with new ones. Nicodemus (John 3) found this to be his
problem; so incredible to believe and so difficult to do. Buttrick's
formula is pertinent for one's whole ministry: "Pastoral work
builds a congregation; preaching holds it." It is not enough,
moreover, to challenge them. The preacher must encourage
them and draw them along. Someone has said, "Encourage
them in their goodness rather than condemn them for their bad-
ness." Scolding gets nowhere. What is more, the preacher must
have the confidence of the people before she or he can persuade.
Bunyan in The Pilgrim's Progress finds in the House of the Interpreter a portrait of the ideal pastor: "His eyes were lifted up to
heaven; the world was behind his back; the best of books was in
his hand; and he stood as if he pleaded with men."[5]

Among the writings of the ancient Greek and Roman orators
we find what great store they laid upon the art of persuasion.
Aristotle, Plato, and Cicero brought strong emphasis upon the
persuasive factor into their theories of rhetoric. Take Plato, for

example, in *The Phaedrus:* he specified good speaking depends
upon the speaker knowing the truth of the subject on which she
or he speaks; effective persuasion is based on knowing the truth;
effective speaking requires proper arrangement and organization; every speaker must know human character; an effective
speaker must know the methods and means by which the hearer
is affected or influenced; and an orator must have a moral
purpose—to make the will of God prevail.

The word "charisma" emerges in any discussion of persuasion
in preaching. What is charisma? Some feel it is difficult to define
because they conclude that some people have it and others do
not. The truth is, however, that many permit their charisma to
remain underdeveloped. David H. C. Read ventured a definition: "It is an elusive quality of charm, personal magnetism, and
personal power, the capacity to excite one's fellow men." But the
average person retorts and says, "OK, but if you have not been
born with this, you cannot manufacture it. Some preachers have
it and some do not. Norman V. Peale has it, but our preacher has
the personality of a slug." This, however, is a limited interpretation of charisma. According to the New Testament, charisma
means: to be spiritually dynamic, which is the key to initiating
action in others; to be so sensitive to the Gospel that it brings
about through you what it promises; to be so vital with new life
that you exert a contagion that affects others. Charisma is not
the product of a Madison Avenue finishing school or cosmetics
shop. It is, as Read added, "The gift of God that flows from his
grace; and grace is everything Christ means to those who know
him."

BE PROPHETIC

No preaching can be truly effective unless it is prophetic.
What do we mean by prophetic preaching? Historically speaking the Christian preacher is the successor to the Old Testament
prophet. As Forsyth wrote, "The Christian preacher is not the
successor of the Greek orator, but of the Hebrew prophet. The

orator comes with but an inspiration; the prophet comes with a revelation."[6] You and I may learn from the Greek and Roman orators how to affect and persuade an audience, but as preachers we are not their successors. We are in debt to them technique-wise, but our identity is with the Hebrew prophets.

What is meant by prophetic preaching? It is easier to say what it does not mean.

It does not mean merely foretelling events such as predicting the day or the hour when the world will end. It is not a matter of presuming that you have some particular inside information because you have a special leased wire to the court of heaven. Unfortunately this is the thrust of a lot of phony evangelism with its strident sermon topic "Millions Now Living Will Never Die."

It does not mean that some preachers have a special gift for interpreting signs, such as the meaning of 666 or who will be among the 144,000 surrounding God's throne on the day of judgment. It may mean that a preacher is competent to interpret national and sociological events and trends, but it does not imply, as Reinhold Niebuhr quipped, that you can measure the temperature of hell or describe the furniture of heaven.

It does not mean that any preacher among us is called to be a herald of doom or gloom, one who lashes out at the congregation with threats of dire consequences. Robert Burns described the parson of his ancestral church ascending the pulpit steps "with tidings o' damnation."

It does not mean—at the other extreme—that everything will be fine regardless. God does not wear continually the smile of a Cheshire cat, nor promise to everyone "pie in the sky by and by."

The High Commissioner to Canada from Guyana remarked, "The Old Testament prophets did not merely tell the future: that is palmistry. They offered people the options of the hour and the moral implications of those options."

What, then, is meant by being prophetic in one's preaching? One possible definition is: to declare an "ought-ness" for living over against the "is-ness" of life. It is a confrontation or encounter of life as the Bible indicates it ought to be with life as women and men live it on their own. The important word here ought to be "relevance." Relevance makes the preacher's task twofold: she or he must explain and interpret this "ought-ness" so the people will understand; and she or he must uncover or expose their human "is-ness" so they can see that their real need is redemption. This means not merely showing women and men *what* they are, but *who* they are, that is, their significance and worth in the eyes of God. Remember John Masefield's poem "The Everlasting Mercy" in which the drunken galoot, Saul Kane, was converted, and in that tremendous awakening he suddenly learned "what I was worth to God." Incidentally, the remark "making the Word of God or the Gospel relevant to the world" makes no sense. The New Testament is evidence that the Word has already been made relevant to the world and it is our business as preachers to explain and interpret it so that its meaning for the people becomes clear.

This constant tension between "ought-ness" and "is-ness" is one of the basic features of prophetic preaching. Christian preaching must not ever consist of making parallel descriptions of what is the nature of God and what is the nature of humankind, but in something of that spiritual dynamic and ferment that is set up by the interaction of the two. Hear Jesus in the synagogue at Nazareth when he declared: "The Spirit of the Lord is upon me, because he has anointed me to preach good news to the poor. He has sent me to proclaim release to the captives and recovering of sight to the blind, to set at liberty those who are oppressed, to proclaim the acceptable year of the Lord" (Luke 4:18). Here is the Word of God (a vertical line) intersecting our common human existence (a horizontal line). Lesslie Newbigin, formerly of the Church of South India, defined salvation as "the mending of that which is broken; the healing of that which was wounded; and the setting at liberty them that are bound." The preacher's task is ever the same: to proclaim that the means to realize this salvation, namely, the everlasting Word, is already here.

Epilogue:
The Ultimate Identity
(John 20:19-22)

It was the evening of the first Christian Sunday. And what a day it had been! The scene was probably the upper room where a group of the disciples were—as Alexander Maclaren said—"eagerly discussing what had happened that day." All sorts of unusual reports were in the air: the incident of the women at the tomb; the experiences of Peter and John; and the strange encounter of the two pedestrians on the Emmaus road. Moreover, these things were enveloped by an atmosphere of fear. After all, with the success of the civic and temple authorities in rubbing out their Leader, the disciples themselves could easily become the victims of guilt by association and be subject to harassment and arrest.

Then a most extraordinary thing happened: the return of the crucified Jesus became in their presence a living reality. Think of what this strange appearance must have meant and done to these fearing and incredulous disciples. The most unique and unprecedented event in all of human history broke upon their consciousness—a human individual risen from the dead!

There was more, however. Their Master, who had been done to death scarcely three days before, was alive and among them again, but in something of a twofold sense. Certainly his familiar voice identified him: "Peace be unto you!" How often had they heard and known that blessing in the past! Yet, another feature was dominant: the triumphant spirit of this once-human Jesus was freed now to be there and everywhere present throughout all ages. He was now indisputably Savior and Lord.

This appearance, moreover, was not an end in itself. Something creative and purposeful was going into action. From noon on Friday until Sunday morning everything had been in disarray. Was this collapse of things to continue? Would Peter really go back to fishing? Would Matthew return to collecting excise taxes? Was it now all over—these three years of training and fellowship with the greatest religious genius of all time? Seemingly, and for the moment, yes. A dispirited group of Jesus followers were now dangling in a state of passivity without any focus whatsoever and, deprived of Jesus' pivotal presence, they had no real identity of their own. But then came the rallying pronouncement: "As the Father has sent me, even so send I you." Their calling was to become crystallized by these words and the direction of their mission was to revolve around who they now were. Their identification came from no other source or authority than from Jesus himself and it would be sustained by the continuity of their experience of that new life in and from him.

It has never been an uncommon question for people, even church members, to ask, Who are these Christian disciples? ministers of God's Word? servants of Christ? What is their identity?

Their identity became clear when they merged themselves with Christ in the Christian enterprise. "As the Father has sent me," said Jesus, "even so send I you." To throw oneself into the work and witness of the Christian community is to be identified with Christ and to become allied with the purpose God entrusted to God's Son. What is more, what God achieved for humankind in Christ must now through voluntary surrender to him be wrought out and completed in all men and women everywhere. "Even so send I you" urges every Christian disciple toward continuous action. Outward living must proclaim Christ's life in them. Their marks of identification were "lights in the world," "salt of the earth," "leaven in the meal," "springs of living water," and so on. And what was still more, the "sent" must pattern themselves after the Sender and this spelt totality. Christ asks for their all—body, soul, and spirit—all that they

have, are, and hope to be; that is, all that God's grace can make
of them and enable them to become. Someone asked General
William Booth of the Salvation Army to explain the success of his
work and mission and he said, "I will tell you the secret. God had
all there was of me. On that day when I caught a vision of what
Jesus Christ could do with the poor of the land, I made up my
mind that God should have all of William Booth there was. And
if there is any power in the Salvation Army today, it is because
God has had all the adoration of my heart, all the power of my
will, and all the influence of my life."

The identity of the disciples was reflected in the means they
used to fulfill the Christian mission. The fallacy of the old
maxim "the end justifies the means" was exposed when it was
discovered that the means determines invariably the nature and
character of the ends. When the early Christian converts made
forays out into the pagan world, before there was any organized
church, their means and methods of action were so novel and
different that the common people asked, "Who are these?" They
seemed bent upon mission and wherever they went what they
said and did excited either curiosity or animosity. "These men
who have turned the world upside down have come here also"
(Acts 17:6). They performed healings, declared God's forgiving-
ness to persons of faith, announced a spiritual kingdom at work
to establish a new type of freedom, and asked for personal loy-
alty to one Jesus of Nazareth who had conquered death and
"brought life and immortality to light through the gospel" (2
Tim. 1:10). Their identity was not that of conquerors with
Roman charioteers; rather they were little-known persons whose
only daring was, "We have the mind of Christ" (1 Cor. 2:16).
Stoned, imprisoned, railed against, lied about—they imitated
their Master well ever since before these disciples "he showed
them his hands and his side." They, too, were servants of the
Word. They wore the marks of discipleship (cf. Paul's words in
Gal. 6:17). Identifying themselves with human sin, they exem-
plified the forgiven life of those who took up their cross and followed Christ.

What about the preacher and the Christian mission today? There are two types of identification and they are allied with the means each witness chooses. There is the identification that is assumed. Its lodestar is a tradition, an organization that is deified, a security based upon material assets, a position buttressed by dogmas or creeds, a "sent-ness" that muddies the means and therefore fails to clarify or realize where to go with what. There is the identification that is derived, the result of declaring and exhibiting the good news from the Sender by the sent and accomplishing a meeting between the Word and the people. The true and faithful preacher has a grasp of the Bible through years of academic and theological training; but also, he or she is grasped by the Bible through a personal experience of Jesus Christ, the eternal Word, in their life. Blend these two elements together and the pulpit's priority becomes an unfolding of the acts of God and how such were wrought out in the history and destiny of the human race.

This type of identification exercises a contagion and works a decisive impact. The Word presented with such essentials invariably elicits a response on the part of some who become sharers in God's purpose and will for the world. Gustav Wingren wrote, "Only when I am gripped by the Word of God can I say a word that will grip others." And the means to this end is most efficacious when the preacher as servant of the Word can endorse the message by pointing, figuratively of course, to "his hands and his side."

The disciples' identity became an active principle by virtue of the resources upon which they drew. The disciples were never more definitely nobodies than when they were esconsced behind closed doors. "The doors being shut . . . for fear of the Jews" (John 20:19). Impotence is the enemy of identity. Any delineation of one's calling becomes blurred when a person shrinks from meeting the outside world. But two things occurred that evening in that upper room which made a decisive difference. (1) Jesus showed these cowering disciples "his hands and his side." This proved it was really he, but more: he seemingly declared, "Look what I've been through and you stand there trembling." He, the divine ("who knew no sin," 2 Cor. 5:21), for our sakes identified himself with us and having carried our guilt in and through death he was to become our companion forever in life. (2) Then he equipped them for the Christian mission: "He breathed on them, and said to them, 'Receive the Holy Spirit' " (John 20:22). Now they came out of their anonymity and exercised this new life and influenced others. Maclaren comments, "This is the power that fits any of us for the work for which we are sent into the world. . . . If we are to be Christ's representatives, Christ's life must be in us."[1]

This role could not be fulfilled behind closed doors, nor in isolation from the Christian community. As someone said, "The New Testament knows nothing of a solitary Christian." In the fellowship of the committed, our Christian identity emerges, is nurtured, and matures. A student asked the president of one of our theological seminaries, "Can a Christian be just as good outside the church as in?" The answer came quickly, "The real question for me is whether I am going to be a real, vital, witnessing, believing member of the body of Christ or a parasite cast on the outside, sucking its life and contributing nothing."

Every Christian, whether lay or ordained, is sent into the world, charged with spiritual power, declaring God's Word of forgiveness and mercy, and is known by his or her association with that community of people, the church, who believe in God. The preacher asks, "Who am I?" Jesus responds, "As the Father has sent me, even so send I you." Invariably, this is where one's identity is found.

Notes

CHAPTER 1

1. Daniel Jenkins, *The Gift of Ministry* (London: Faber & Faber, 1947), 12.

2. Ralph Waldo Emerson, *Journal*, quoted by Charles F. Kemp in *Pastoral Preaching* (St. Louis: Bethany Press, 1963), 41, 42.

3. Peter T. Forsyth, *Positive Preaching and the Modern Mind* (Grand Rapids: Wm. B. Eerdmans, 1964), 55.

4. Douglas Webster, *What Is Evangelism?* (London: Highway Press, 1959), 131.

5. Robert A. Guelich, "On Being a Minister of the Word," *Bethel Seminary Journal* 17, no. 5 (1968): 15.

6. Paul Clifford, *The Pastoral Calling* (Great Neck, N.Y.: Channel Press, 1961), 7.

7. Charles S. Duthie, *God in His World* (London: Independent Press, 1954), 88.

8. Forsyth, *Positive Preaching*, 66.

9. Donald Bloesch, "The Need for Biblical Preaching," *The Reformed Journal* 19, no. 1 (1969): 12.

10. Thomas F. Torrance, *Conflict and Agreement in the Church* (London: Lutterworth Press, 1959), 158.

CHAPTER 2

1. John Calvin, *Institutes of the Christian Religion*, trans. Henry Beveridge (Grand Rapids: Wm. B. Eerdmans, 1953), vol. 4, part 1, p. 285.

2. Ibid.

3. Jenkins, *Gift of Ministry*, 23.

4. Walter J. Ong, *The Presence of the Word* (New Haven: Yale University Press, 1967), 1.

5. Ibid., 125.

6. G. Kittel, *Theological Dictionary of the New Testament* (Grand Rapids: Wm. B. Eerdmans, 1967), 4:79–80.

7. Ibid., 97, 98.

8. R. W. Dale, *The Atonement*, 25th ed. (London: Congregational Union of England and Wales, 1909), 107.

9. T. H. L. Parker, *The Oracles of God* (London: Lutterworth Press, 1967), 21.

10. Karl Barth, *The Preaching of the Gospel* (Philadelphia: Westminster Press, 1963), 9, 10.

CHAPTER 3

1. Leroy Nixon, *John Calvin: Expository Preacher* (Grand Rapids: Wm. B. Eerdmans, 1950), 57.

2. Harry Emerson Fosdick, "What Is the Matter with Preaching?" *Harpers* (June 1928): 25.

3. William A. Quale, *The Pastor-Preacher*, ed. W. W. Wiersbe (Grand Rapids: Baker Book House, 1979), 27.

4. Reuel Howe, *The Miracle of Dialogue* (Greenwich, Conn.: Seabury Press, 1963), 58.

5. Expanded on in chap. 3 of Barth, *Preaching of the Gospel*, 56–66.

6. See Theodore Ferris's paragraph on "dryness" in *Go Tell the People* (New York: Charles Scribner's Sons, 1951), 100–105.

7. Forsyth, *Positive Preaching*, 53.

8. John Calvin, *Predigten über das 2. Buch Samuelis* (Neukirchen: Erziehungsvereins, 1936), 136.

9. Joseph Sittler, *The Ecology of Faith* (Philadelphia: Muhlenberg Press, 1961), 73.

10. Jenkins, *Gift of Ministry*, 34.

CHAPTER 4

1. Phillips Brooks, *Lectures on Preaching* (London: SPCK, 1959), 77.

2. Harry Emerson Fosdick, quoted by Robert M. Miller in *Harry Emerson Fosdick: Preacher, Pastor, Prophet* (New York: Oxford University Press, 1985), 345.

3. Harry Emerson Fosdick, "How I Prepare My Sermons," in *Harry Emerson Fosdick's Art of Preaching*, ed. Lionel George Crocker (Springfield, Ill.: Charles C. Thomas, 1971), 44.

4. William Law, *A Serious Call to a Devout and Holy Life* (Philadelphia: Westminster Press, 1948), 197.

5. George Matheson, "Make Me a Captive, Lord," in *The Hymnbook*, ed. David H. Jones (Philadelphia: Presbyterian Church in the USA, 1955), 264.

6. Francis Thompson, "The Hound of Heaven," in *Modern English Poetry*, ed. Louis Untermeyer (New York: Harcourt, Brace & Co., 1930), 247.

CHAPTER 5

1. Richard Borden, *Public Speaking—as Listeners Like It* (New York: Harper & Brothers, 1935), 3.

2. Frederick B. Speakman, *The Salty Tang* (Westwood, N.J.: Fleming H. Revell, 1954), passim.

3. Herbert H. Farmer, "The Preacher and Persons," *Review and Expositor* 43 (1946): 411.

4. J. C. Shairp, "Prose Poets: Cardinal Newman," in *Aspects of Poetry* (London: Oxford University Press, 1881), 444.

5. John Bunyan, *The Pilgrim's Progress* (London: SCM Press, 1947), 42.

6. Forsyth, *Positive Preaching*, 1.

EPILOGUE

1. Alexander Maclaren, "The Gospel of St. John," in *Expositions of Holy Scripture* (Grand Rapids: Wm. B. Eerdmans, 1952), 314–15.

LINCOLN CHRISTIAN COLLEGE AND SEMINARY

DA